EP Sport Se

W9-BWD-171

* All About J
* Badminton
* Basketball
  Competitive Swimming
  Conditioning for Sport
  Cricket
  Field Athletics
* Football
* Golf
  Hockey for Men and Women
  Improve your Riding
  Learning to Swim
  Men's Gymnastics
  Modern Riding
* Netball
* Orienteering
  Rock Climbing
  Sailing
* Snooker
* Squash Rackets
  Start Motor Cruising
* Table Tennis
* Tennis up to Tournament
    Standard
* Track Athletics
  Underwater Swimming
  Volleyball
  Wildwater Canoeing
  Women's Gymnastics

At the time of publication of this
edition the asterisked titles are
available in paperback as well as
hardback

 EP PUBLISHING LIMITED

ep sport

competitive swimming

hamilton bland

Acknowledgements

All the photographs in this book were taken by Tony Duffy.

The cover and frontispiece show David Parker, bronze medallist in the 1975 World Championships, and coached by the author.

ISBN 0 7158 0603 3 (cased)
ISBN 0 7158 0656 4 (limp)

Published by EP Publishing Ltd, East Ardsley, Wakefield, West Yorkshire, 1979

Text set in 11/12 pt Monophoto Univers, printed by photolithography and bound in Great Britain by G. Beard & Son Ltd, Brighton, Sussex

About the author

After completing his course at Loughborough College, Hamilton Bland taught for two years at Rugby School. In both 1968 and 1972 he was a British Olympic Coach, and in 1969 he won a Winston Churchill Scholarship. Currently he is chief coach for the City of Coventry Swimming Club and General Secretary of the British Swimming Coaches Association. Hamilton Bland combines this with work as a BBC TV swimming commentator.

Contents

Introduction

Competitive swimming benefits considerably from the thousands of young children taught to swim annually in swimming clubs. This never-ending supply of clientèle provides vast numbers of potential competitors, which few, if any other sport, can boast. An added advantage is that many of these children are under eleven, attracted to the sport before any other sport has 'had the chance' to lay out its stall! The needs of learning to swim for survival quickly progress to the needs of competition; indeed, the strokes as taught have been designed and regulated for competition purposes. 'Correct breast stroke and backstroke' etc., are not necessarily the most efficient ways of swimming on the front and back, but simply legal methods acceptable in competition. Although races are held for younger children, it is internationally accepted that ten years is about the correct age for competition to begin. At this age it is important that the skills of the sport are stressed and perhaps the established practice of providing only short sprint-type races should be discouraged. Events in which good starting, timing and, most important of all, good stroking, are emphasised, should be encouraged. The bigger, stronger children will always win the more power-like sprint events, and, therefore, events at say 200 m should perhaps be held as these would not be won on purely physical grounds as is the case with the sprints.

As learning to swim and correct the strokes develops into training for competition at about ten years of age, so more time is required for practice. At this age something like three sessions of approximately one hour will be necessary and should be adequate for most needs.

Competitions are organised locally, regionally and nationally in most countries in age groups and these are normally grouped as '11 and Unders', '12s and 13s', '14s and 15s' and '16s and 17s' or, as is becoming the fashion, 'born 1967 and after', 65/66, 63/64, 61/62. Age-group competitions emerged from the USA and have done a great deal to improve the various motivations required en route to senior swimming. It has, however, got its fair share of drawbacks. The major drawback has already been mentioned: especially in the younger age groups it is often the bigger, stronger children who succeed, being aided by the sprint-type competitions offered. This of course discourages smaller children and many retire before reaching even their teens! At about fourteen, in the girls' case, and fifteen or sixteen with the boys, there is a levelling off of this previous physical advantage, and at this stage it is the swimmers who are better technically and have conditioned themselves through training, who succeed. The great pity of the sport is the number of children lost to it as a result of this age-group system and children supposedly not 'making it' at eleven and twelve years of age!

Training and Rewards

Once training has begun the demands required by the sport will begin to emerge. Competitive swimming does probably demand more training time than any other sport. Already two or three one-hour sessions at ten years of age has been mentioned. At the top of the scale, senior international swimmers will probably spend ten or eleven two-hour sessions (or more) in the pool each week, covering sixty miles and over! One of the problems that the swimmer is faced with is just how to get this amount of training in and go to school or to work. The answer is, of course, to swim early in the morning and it is universally accepted now that in order to compete effectively at almost any level, this will be necessary. The international standard swimmers often swim five early mornings from six until eight while the 10s and 11s may only swim one early morning for perhaps sixty minutes and progress to more mornings if and when they improve. It has surprised many parents and teachers just how quickly children adapt to this routine, and one thing is certain — if they didn't want to do it then they wouldn't! This in itself, however, does not make it right and one of the coach's great decisions is to determine just how many early mornings a child should undertake. The demands are also parental ones; the swimmers have to be taken to the pool each session, certainly each early-morning session when it is highly unlikely that public transport will be available. Swimming is a physically exhausting sport involving all muscles of the body as well as the heart and lungs; and, as a result, a sixty-minute session can be a very demanding period. This will have to be doubled or even trebled and repeated ten or eleven times per week, over a period of a number of years if the child is to succeed nationally and internationally. It is obviously very time-consuming, and one of the reasons why swimmers reach international standards in their early teens is that this is when they have most time for training before the demands of

exams, college, university or work are presented. Other reasons include the fact that by the time swimmers reaches fourteen or fifteen they will have probably been training seriously for four or five years; and finally, in many of the events, complete physical maturity is not a prerequisite for success because only in the sprints is strength all-important. These are the reasons that world records, particularly in the distance events, have been broken by thirteen-year-old girls and fifteen-year-old boys. The demands, therefore, are varied and strenuous and are present over a number of years. Patience is an essential quality for the swimmer to possess, as is a realistic outlook as to what gains can reasonably be expected from the sport. In order to succeed, the swimmer will have to attend frequently, be punctual and work hard when in the pool! If the swimmer ensures that there is no deficiency in these aspects of training, then the coach has a chance. If the swimmer misses sessions or is often late or does not try hard enough during training, then neither the ability of the coach nor the

swimmer is being measured and an awful lot of time is being wasted.
The rewards of competing in this sport are as varied and even more long term than the demands of it. Probably the greatest reward of all is the carry-over that the discipline of training requires into other aspects of the swimmer's life. Swimmers have to be disciplined in so many ways in terms of attendance and punctuality along with sustained effort. Many top swimmers display these same characteristics and succeed at school in exams and after school in work. Their lives are well organised. Homework has to be done at a certain time in a certain time and, consequently, is done; and, in the case of a swimmer having success in swimming, is also done well. Many teachers and parents have observed that when a child is swimming well his or her schoolwork is good and vice versa. Many swimming coaches demand that the child cuts training if schoolwork suffers, which often has a very good effect. If a child cannot afford ninety minutes or so each evening to

take part in his or her chosen hobby or sport because of school homework then it is most likely that the child has been incorrectly placed or, and more uncommonly, the school is being unreasonable with the amount of homework set. Obviously there are academic pressure periods such as revising and actual examination times that will have to be catered for and this is done in all effective training situations. To be successful, swimmers must be well organised and in gaining this quality they are being well equipped indeed for future life.

The obvious early rewards come from learning to swim the first few strokes and then passing on to swimming the first width and length. Motivation at this stage is no problem. Thereafter, the demands, the relative rewards and necessary motivation should be carefully controlled. Having learned to swim a distance for survival purposes, the next incentive should be to learn to swim well. This means spending time perfecting strokes so that any bad habits that have been established can be quickly eradicated. Once the strokes have been mastered the emphasis may be put on speed, with good, correct stroke, and not before. Badges are available for all these stages, 'I can swim one length', 'I can swim good backstroke' etc., and will provide the extra motivation so necessary. As well as taking part in competitions, badges are also available to be won to indicate on a national basis just how fast the swimmer can swim while complying with the rules. These awards, which are most attractive, can be worn on track suits and are obvious rewards for all the effort put in. The greatest reward of all in the pool is, of course, to win the race, whether it be the novice one length or the Olympic Final. The culmination of all the effort is there for all to see.

Parents and Coach

The role of the swimmer has already been partly covered and will be completed in the following pages of this book. The role of the parent, a most difficult one indeed, has been touched upon. The parent has two extreme options of involvement: either total — getting involved in the club, sitting on committees, watching every training session and going to every competition, or, relatively low-level involvement — simply acting as chauffeur and sponsor along with, of course, giving the necessary encouragement when required. Both parental approaches have been successful and unsuccessful. What really matters is what approach is going to suit the parent *in the honest, best and real interests of the child*. The problem that faces most swimming parents is that they enter the sport knowing absolutely nothing about it and understandably, because of the time and money that they spend in the sport, they are anxious for rewards, whether it be reflected glory as a result of the club doing well, or satisfaction in the fact that the child is involved in a worthwhile activity. They are never in the sport for very long, the vast majority only as long as their children are competing. This means that they really do not have time to develop a real long-term and in-depth knowledge of the sport. Whereas the coach will be ultimately interested in the swimmer reaching national and international level, mum and dad are really interested in tomorrow's success. The coach will have to understand this and will have to be able to deal with not only swimmer frustration but also parental frustration when things do not seem to be happening quickly enough. Parents must really believe in the coach, just as the swimmer will have to. If the coach is consulted, not on a daily basis of course, then if he is 'doing the job', he should very easily be able to explain the stage of development reached and his hopes for the future, and should be only too willing to pass this information on if it is requested. To contribute positively to the swimmer's progress the 'ideal parent' will have to be encouraging, patient and coach-informed.

The role of the coach is certainly the most difficult one. He or she will probably be personally directing the complete swimming progress of about thirty or so swimmers. Most of his duties are obvious. However, to be really effective and consequently successful, the coach will have to be skilful at continually motivating the swimmers while applying just the correct amount of pressure during training, in treating each of his squad as an individual. This requires careful observation by the coach and will involve a lot of discussion between coach and swimmer about the progress made and the immediate and long-term aims of the programme. The coach will be responsible for directing the remaining content of this book and his or her skill at doing this will be reflected in the results gained by the swimmers in competition. There are many ideal qualities that the coach should possess; the most important of these are complete reliability and a real determination to succeed. On the whole swimmers are as good as they believe and as good as their coaches can make them believe. Many swimmers change coaches because they believe the coach at the next pool is a better one and it is often this belief alone that makes them swim better, nothing else.

As one would expect, then, there are many factors that combine to ensure that a swimmer will be successful. The swimmer himself or herself will have to put in a lot of effort supported by the parents in just the right way and directed by the coach with all his skill. It will also help to be a member of a well-organised club. The club will make all the necessary competition entries and will also probably help finance some of the competitive involvement once the swimmer reaches a certain level. The most successful clubs also employ professional coaches which means that swimmers only have to pay moderately for these essential services.

Medical Considerations

Swimming clubs often have associated with them a doctor who has a particular interest in the sport. Every swimmer will of course have his or her own general practitioner to whom all complaints should initially be directed. The general practitioner's advice should be strictly adhered to at all times. If a swimming club does engage the services of a 'club doctor', he or she will know exactly how to liaise with the family doctor, hospitals, etc. The club doctor should be encouraged to work on the poolside if possible in order that he or she might become familiar with the many types of ailments that swimmers encounter and how these affect the swimmer in training and competition. It is vital that 'swimming injuries' are understood by whoever is treating them and that the correct treatment is given. 'Correct' in this context means the best treatment available that will allow the swimmer to recommence training as quickly as possible.

Every swimmer should have a routine medical check-up, including a chest x-ray, at least once each year and preferably before a period of intensive training. In addition to this should be a regular dental check. Nothing will be more conducive to upsetting the preparation than a bout of toothache near to the event. The purpose of this section of the book is not to explain how to treat every ache and pain but simply to make the various ailments known and to suggest just how they might affect the training programme.

Swimmers, like any other group of people, will suffer from the common cold, sinusitis and various forms of ear infections. Constantly having to get wet then dry and move from the warm indoors to the cold outside will of course, if the swimmer is not very careful, result in these common ailments occurring very frequently. All of these relatively minor complaints should be treated with a great deal of respect and the swimmer should aim to get rid of them completely, but naturally, as quickly as possible.

The other most frequent complaints are those of athlete's foot and verrucae. Athlete's foot is a condition that often occurs between the toes when the skin becomes white and begins to peel. There are several causes of this, weating and irritation of the ocks being just two of them. wimmers suffering from a mild orm of this can treat it with ne of the many powders or intments on the market. This an develop into an extremely ainful and serious complaint nd therefore if early treatment s not successful a doctor hould be visited. It will always elp if the swimmer dries the eet thoroughly, particularly etween the toes, after wimming and adds a little lusting powder. Verrucae are ngrowing warts and can easily e caught if the swimmer valks around unnecessarily and arelessly without shoes on. Should a verruca be contracted t should be treated mmediately by a chiropodist orivately or at a hospital. They ire contagious and consequently should be emoved completely before the swimmer is allowed to ecommence training. Swimmers will at times experience aching in the various muscles. This will occur after a lay-off period or after a heavy training period. These iches will normally disappear naturally although some heat reatment and massage will of course speed up the process. They should not interfere with the training programme to any real degree.

Girl swimmers will also have to deal with their monthly periods. Many Olympic Medals have been won by girls who were actually menstruating and the condition should be treated exactly as it is—a natural occurrence. Most girls use an internal tampon and experience no real problems. Some do have acute muscle ache and the coach, if informed, will make allowances for this.

Cramp is a condition that most swimmers experience at some time in their careers and is a very painful one. The exact reasons for its being brought on are not known. Many believe that a lack of salt in the body is an important contributing factor. Cramp is often experienced in the calf muscles immediately after push-off and over-contraction of the calf muscles. If the swimmer is allowed a short rest cramp will normally go away quite naturally. Warm water often speeds up the recovery. If a swimmer appears to be pale or easily gets tired in training then anaemia could be the problem. This is a condition easy to diagnose by a doctor and relatively easy to treat. Coaches should be on the look-out for symptoms of it. Another common ailment is known as breaststroker's knee. The unnatural nature of the movement puts unusual pressures on the tendons and ligaments of the joint and often results in slight.damage of some fibres which naturally brings with it some pain. The only cure for this is rest or at least a change from breast-stroke kick. This rest will allow the fibres to mend. In order that no recurrence takes place, or to prevent it from happening in the first place, breast stroke and breast-stroke kick should be planned in the session very carefully. A short dry-land warm-up consisting of easy knee-bending exercises followed by some gentle breast-stroke kicking should be all that is necessary.

No special foods should be necessary as long as the swimmers have a well-balanced diet. The doctor may, however, recommend some vitamin-type supplement should he feel it would be beneficial. This could well be the case if the

13

swimmer becomes involved in a long intensive-training period. The obvious detriments to health such as alcohol, smoking, lack of sleep, etc., should be avoided. Swimmers will vary as to how much sleep they need but none of them will require cigarettes, cigars, pipes or alcohol.

At international level it is commonplace to see physiotherapists at work with swimmers. Much of their value lies in the psychological calming down that they are able to bring about while massaging the swimmers before the race. They will of course also be able to treat any muscle injury should it occur. Finally, as most clubs do now take part in competition, certain vaccinations will be necessary and these must be completed at the best times that will again least affect training or competition. The 'normal' ones include smallpox, polio, cholera and typhoid. The club doctor or general practitioner will again advise on these matters.

It is vital that the swimmer keeps as well as possible at all times. Many aspects of the sport are not conducive to this. Having to swim twice or three times each day for up to six hours, moving from the warm swimming pool to the often cold outdoors, are just some of the conditions that have to be accepted if the swimmer is to succeed.

For apparently quite a simple sport a good deal of equipment will in fact be required. The piece of equipment necessary for training that should be present in the pool at all training times is **the training clock** – a large sweephand affair that is visible on starting and finishing to both swimmer and coach. This is used to start swimmers off in the first instance; the coach might say 'first swimmers go on "sixty" and the rest at five-second intervals'. It is also used for pace judgement, with the swimmer glancing up at the clock during the swim, and of course for timing the swim. This frees the coach from having to say 'go' several hundred times each hour and from timing or attempting to time every swimmer every swim. He will, of course, check some times occasionally on his stop watch. Many pools have two such training clocks, especially the 50 m ones. **Lane lines** should also be put in during every training session. Competition lane lines are now at a very advanced stage of design and are said to be 'antiturbulence lines'. A series of plastic discs about 5 in (125 mm) in diameter and 1 in (25 mm) wide are threaded along the nylon line and these spin as the water laps against them, thus breaking down the small waves that are made by the swimmer. Many new pools, and certainly those intended for

high-level competition, are called **deck level**. These pools are designed so that the water surface is level with the pool side and allows the water to lap over on to the side and down a channel situated close to it.

This type of pool design together with antiturbulence lines makes for a perfect, flat racing surface. **Starting blocks** are also essential during some training sessions in order that the necessary skills of starting, as outlined

later, can be mastered. A good starting block is inclined to the front, has backstroke starting handle or handles, and has a front edge that can be gripped by the swimmer if need be. The surface should be non-slip.

Backstroke flags are situated 5 m from the pool ends and are normally about 5 ft (1.5 m) above the water. They are intended to assist the backstroker in siting the end wall and should be used in training when necessary. The **false start rope** is situated

about 25 ft (7.6 m) from the starting end and it is recommended that a 'quick-release' type be employed if possible.

Electronic timing is now being installed in many pools around the country and obviously helps both the swimmers and the judges to obtain an accurate result in a tight or, for that matter, any other type of finish. Fully automatic systems are the best. These are started from the starter's pistol and stopped by the swimmer touching a pad at the finish. Semi-automatic systems are started by each lane timekeeper pressing a button and are stopped in the same way. The best systems are linked to an automatic read-out display so that as each swimmer touches, his or her lane number, position and time are displayed for all to see. All these systems time to one-thousandth of a second but International Law states that the result can only be decided to a one-hundredth of a second. If two swimmers have the same time to 1/100 of a second, therefore, the result is a tie.

Starting blocks

The starter is shown 3 m from the end in an elevated position; his gun activates the electronic timing apparatus

...mekeepers are now making ...ood use of the excellent **ectronic stop watches** ...hich give readings to 1/100 ... a second in a clear, readable ...shion. They also have the ...dded advantage of working ...ut split times and the ability ... totalise these splits ...utomatically.

...nally, **lap cards** are essential ...r 800 m and 1500 m races ...nd are normally numbered 1 ... 30. Usual practice is to ...dicate number of lengths to ...o and this will be done unless ...ther arrangements are made ...etween swimmer and lap ...ounter. A bell or whistle ...ormally indicates that the ...wimmer has two lengths to ...o.

...n addition to these 'permanent ...xtures' or racing and training ...ems of equipment, the ...wimmer will also need ...ersonal equipment. The most ...bvious piece of equipment ...ill of course be the **swim ...uit** itself. The major ...anufacturers now have a ...uperb variety of styles and ...olours to suit every possible ...aste. Style of course is ...ssential to swimmers if they ...re going to produce their best ...ossible times. Men's suits

should be well cut around the leg and ladies' suits should allow full movement of the arms and shoulders and should not allow water to pass down the front or the back. There are several brand and trade names used to describe the various advanced materials of which the suits are made. Basically, the modern materials keep friction down to a minimum and thus prevent drag. One final thing to remember with regard to swim suits is that the suit should be changed immediately after the warm-up and after the heats. A number of suits will, therefore, be required. Nylon suits are used for training and the 'specials' for competition.

The next most important piece of swimming equipment are **anti-chlorine goggles**. These small plastic goggles were first introduced at the Mexico

◀ Frank Pfutze (East Germany),
former European 1500 m record-
holder, seen here wearing anti-
chlorine goggles

Olympic Games of 1968 and
are now to be seen on many
bathers both at the seaside and
at the swimming pool, as well
as on the competitive swimmer.
The main advantages that they
offer to the swimmer are that
(i) poor water conditions such
as too much or too little
chlorine can now be coped
with and swimmers do not have
to leave the pool during
training because of eye
complaints; (ii) swimmers can
see clearly the opposition on
each side with the face in the
water; and (iii) the clarifying
effect on the water of the
goggles makes training and
competing a much more
pleasant experience for the
swimmer. A note of warning,
however, about goggles should
be added and this relates to the
potential danger of them when
they are misused. Correct
procedures are now included
with all goggles sold and
emphasise the correct way of
putting them on, adjusting
them and taking them off. The
coach will find that goggles
provide a convenient excuse for
stopping during training,
particularly when it gets
difficult, in order to adjust
them, etc. The good coach will

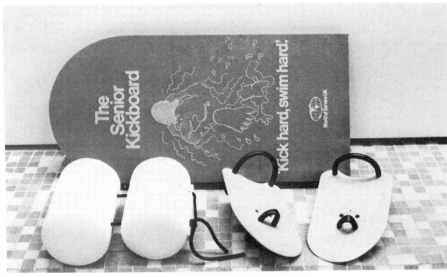

Swimming kickboard (back), pull buoy and hand paddles

not under any circumstances
allow this to happen – as
indeed neither will the good
swimmer!
Other useful items of
equipment are **ear plugs** for
those swimmers who suffer
from minor ear complaints. A
malleable plasticine-type
substance has been developed
which seems to seal the ear
most effectively. **Swimming
floats** or **kickboards**, as they
are now called, are vital pieces
of equipment for the serious
swimmer. The large com-
petitive floats about 15–18 in
(380–450 mm) long and

8–12 in (200–300 mm) wide
are ideal for training purposes.
In order to do arms-only
effectively the **pull buoy** is
used to immobilise the legs
while keeping the body in a
good, flat position. Pull buoys
are not used perhaps as much
as they should be. They are
made up of two sections of
cylindrical high-density foam
about 9 in (230 mm) long and
4 in (100 mm) in diameter,
which fit between the thighs,
one at the front and one at the
back. They are held together
with a piece of nylon and make
for a very effective aid. **Hand**

paddles are invaluable to the swimmer in assisting to increase strength and endurance while also acting as stroke correctors. They are made of slightly malleable plastic and are greater in area than the flat hand, but similar in shape. They are worn on the palm and fingers and are normally held on by two slim rubber tubes which pass through holes in the paddles. The second finger normally passes through the top loop after the hand itself has passed through the wrist-securing loop. It is important that the paddle is not so hard that it becomes dangerous, that full wrist flexion is possible, and that the paddle itself is designed correctly. By wearing these during training, a swimmer can increase his or her strength by swimming the strokes as normal but in the process having to deal with the extra resistance presented by the paddle. The muscles that are strengthened are those specifically used in the arm actions of the various strokes, which means that unnecessary bulk, as often results from a general weight-training programme, is avoided. The

International swimmers, Joy Beasley (left) and Liz Taylor, warmly dressed prior to an important competition

stroke correction comes from the swimmer literally being able to feel what action is necessary when wearing the paddles. This can be likened to wearing flippers which indicate to the swimmer very clearly that the toes should be pointed for maximum effect. So, with the paddles the swimmer is directed towards pressing the hand and forearm backwards for maximum forward propulsion.

The final items of equipment that the competitive swimmer will require include a track suit, tee shirts and socks which should all be warm, as it is essential that the body is kept so before races. A number of towels and a pair of training shoes will also help!

Simple Mechanics

It is essential that swimmers and coaches have at least a basic knowledge of the mechanics involved in their sport. This understanding will enable them to analyse and consider any new styles or suggested stroke adjustments in a sensible manner in order that they will not be led into simply copying someone or something because it is successful.

The science of hydrodynamics is, however, a very detailed one where effective measurement, because of the water, is extremely difficult. What the swimmer and coach are really concerned with are the areas of propulsion and resistance that affect the swimmer in the water.

Propulsion

In 1680 Sir Isaac Newton stated that 'Action and Reaction are equal and opposite.' This phrase is probably the most useful statement that the swimmer and coach will find when considering how the various strokes should be performed.

If the swimmer applies a force backwards then propulsion forwards will result. Related to the arm actions of the four strokes this means that in the **backstroke** the hand and forearm should move backwards for maximum effect. This implies a bent elbow action which is described in the chapter on 'The Strokes' (see page 62). In **breast stroke** once again the hands and forearms should attempt to move backwards if an effective pull is to be executed. Details are given on page 65, but it will be seen that it is a long cry from the pressing out to the side and down that was a common feature of the stroke not long ago. **Freestyle** and **butterfly** have very similar hand- and arm-movement patterns that satisfy the mechanical principles already mentioned. In order to apply a force backwards in these two strokes it is necessary to bend the elbow. The diagram below explains why this is so.

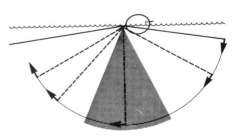

Straight-arm pull

The straight-arm pull on freestyle gives a downwards force during the early part of the pull and an upwards force during the latter part of the movement—the push phase. The downwards pressure will only serve to lift the shoulders and the upward pressure will force the shoulders downwards. The only effective part of this type of pull is that which occurs when the arm is under the body and pressing backwards. This is known as the 'middle range' of movement (shaded).

What has to be developed is a movement that will allow the hand to apply a force backwards for a greater period. This is done by bending the elbow as shown in the diagram below.

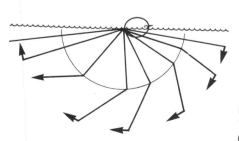

Bent-arm pull

The degree to which the arm is bent depends on both the strength of the swimmer and the event to be swum. As a very general rule the sprint events are swum with straighter arms than the distance events, and tall, relatively weak swimmers need to bend their arms more than short, strong swimmers. Again speaking very generally, the tall, weak swimmers tend to be best suited to the distance events where long, bent-arm economical strokes are required, and the short, stocky, strong swimmers are best suited to the sprint events which are best performed by concentrating on a relatively straight-arm pull in the middle range. Because the tall swimmer has to work with a bent-arm pull throughout the full range of the stroke he will perform much fewer strokes than the sprinter who will only be concerned with the middle range. The best swimmers will of course be tall and strong and will work somewhere between these two extremes of range. The 1976 Olympic 100 m freestyle champion was 6 ft 6 in (1.98 m) tall!

Propulsion itself is gained as a result of the hands and feet 'fixing' in the water and the body being levered past that point. This is very much a simplified explanation but will suffice at this level. In freestyle swimming, the hand enters the water, 'fixes' on it, and the arm is used as a lever to move the body over the relatively still hand. This fixing is possible because of tiny whirlpools or vortices being set up which allow the hand and forearm to exert pressure backwards with the hand remaining in this position. In actual fact the hand does move backwards and sideways a little because once the water molecules have this backwards pressure applied to them they themselves begin to move and this area of water is then rendered useless. Consequently the hand moves to find other 'stationary water'. Underwater photography of world-class swimmers displays this slight but noticeable 'feathering' movement.

Probably the best analogy of this principle is with the oarsman who puts the blade of the oar into the water and then heaves on the opposite end. The blade remains still and the boat moves forwards. The

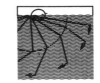

ackstroker performs a very milar action in getting 'hold' the water and levering the ody through it.

he breaststroker gets 'hold' of vo areas of water and presses e body through these. The utterflier in performing almost double freestyle pull gets old' of two areas of water nd levers the body up to, over nd past these areas.

he leg actions of the four trokes are not exempt from the ction and Reaction Law and vill only provide forward ropulsion if they are able to xert a force in the backwards irection. The freestyler ttempts to kick from the hips vith 'long legs', toes pointed s much as possible. There is a light flexing of the knee as the

bottom of the foot reaches the surface of the water on the up-kick. At this point the feet should be hyper-extended. As the down-kick is made so a force is exerted backwards and downwards by the instep and front surface of the lower leg. The foot appears to be moving backwards quite considerably but in fact there is a 'fixing' of the instep on the water which then remains quite still. As the force is applied so the leg straightens and the body moves forwards.

In backstroke the reverse is the case. At the lowest part of the kick the foot is again hyper-extended and the knee is flexed again. This enables the instep and lower leg to apply a force backwards on the *up-kick*. The

same principle of the instep and lower leg 'fixing' on the water applies.

The butterflier performs a double freestyle kick but a much deeper and more effective one. The breaststroker draws the heels up to the seat with the knees quite close and the heels apart. This should be done without allowing the knees to come too far under the body. The feet are then turned outwards, exposing the flat areas of the soles of the feet in addition to the rear of the lower legs facing in a backwards direction. Again, as pressure is then applied, the feet remain quite stationary and allow the legs to straighten and the body to move forwards. The detailed movement is explained on page 67.

Propulsion, then, it can be seen, comes from the application of a force in the opposite direction to that which the swimmer intends to travel. By a system of the hands and feet 'fixing' on the water, the body is able to be levered through it. The exact movement patterns that the limbs actually trace during the strokes are explained in detail on pages 60–77.

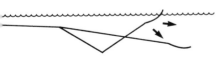

Freestyle kick

Backstroke kick

Resistance

In addition to the considerations of propulsion are the elements of resistance that again are of paramount importance to swimmer and coach.

The first obvious resistance is the *water* itself and the combined advantages of deck-level pools and antiturbulence lane lines, to keep surface movement to a minimum, have already been discussed. The FINA regulation on water temperature is 25°C, about 76–78°F. Anything much above this swimmers find too warm to train and compete in, and any temperature below it is certainly much too cold for efficient performances. Salt water is slightly more buoyant than 'fresh' water and is said by many swimmers to be 'faster' The next most obvious form of resistance is the *body* itself. Its shape is vital if real speed is to be considered. Rowing boats are faster than canoes, given the same paddles and people operating them, because of their shape. The 'ideal' swimmer should be long and slim for best results. The surfaces of the body really presenting resistance to the water and to forwards propulsion are the head, the top of the shoulders, the chest and the back. Obviously all other surfaces offer some degree of resistance but these offer most. Presumably, then, the bigger the head, the broader the shoulders, the larger the chest and back and the slower the swimmer. If this were so, the best swimmer would have a long, pointed head, narrow shoulders, would be flat-chested and hollow-backed! In addition to the torso and the limbs is the resistance of the *hair* on it. Many swimmers now shave their bodies before an important race. This topic is covered in the chapter on tapering and although perhaps the advantages are largely psychological, there is a reduction of friction and resistance as a result.

During the movements of arms and legs necessary to perform the strokes, certain of these *limb positions* and *body positions* also cause resistance to be brought about. The very best limb and body position is with the arms stretched out in front, fingers pointing, head down, body horizontal and legs stretched out behind, toes pointing. Any deviation from this position will cause resistance.

Already swim suits have been mentioned in the personal equipment section. They also will cause resistance, and one of the modern well-designed ones should be used if this is to be kept to a minimum. (See page 19.)

Many of these aspects of resistance may seem to be relatively trivial and unimportant. However, if real success is to be achieved they will have to be respected and decreased to a minimum. It is interesting to observe the yachtsman preparing his craft to give it almost a glass finish to reduce the resistance. This is in stark contrast to some swimmers who spend hours each day in getting fitter and then swim the race in ill-fitting suits or excess body hair.

Starting

Races can be won and lost before the swimmers get wet! The start of the race is of paramount importance and consequently must be performed excellently. The best starters in the world do not try to beat the gun, but on hearing it consistently perform a series of well-practised movements that result in a fast start. The start should be learned in training, and as a result of timing the various starts the one to be employed should be practised under pressure as often as possible.

The method of timing the start is to have a cane projecting over the water about 25 ft (7.6 m) from the starting block in a lane close to the wall. As the gun is fired so the time begins. The watch is stopped as the swimmer's head touches the line underneath the cane. The distance of 25 ft (7.6 m) will just allow the swimmer to surface and will not measure swimming speed as such, but overall starting speed.

The start can be broken down into:

- reaction time, that is the time taken for the first movement to take place after the sound of the start has been heard
- the starting position employed – either the swing, the grab or the track
- the movement from the block
- the flight
- the entry
- the strokes under water and the commencement of full stroking.

All these facets of the start, irrespective of which particular start is employed, should be carefully considered by both coach and swimmer. Obviously reaction time can only be improved upon by constant practice under pressure. The movement from the block should be as fast as possible but should allow the legs to be put into the most advantageous pushing position before the thrust by them is exerted. The flight should be relatively low and very streamlined so that the entry can be made as streamlined as possible also. The feet should aim to pass through the hole made in the water by the hands, with the toes pointing. Certain movements will be necessary by the arms and legs, as discussed in the chapter on 'The Strokes' (see page 60) to bring the body to the surface in order that full stroking can commence. What is vital is that full stroking should not commence before or after maximum swimming speed is achieved. This can only be appreciated as a result of practice. If the swimmer begins to swim too soon then he or she will actually slow down

because dive speed is greater than maximum swimming speed. If the swimmer leaves it too late until getting into full stroke, then there will be a need to accelerate to maximum swimming speed.

The most common start employed by top swimmers is known as the 'grab start'. The swimmer gets into a position with his feet either hip width apart or feet together with the toes gripping the edge of the starting block. The front of the block, which normally has a front face about 2 in (50 mm) deep, is gripped by the swimmer's hands either between the feet or outside the feet if they are together. The head looks down and the knees are bent to about 120 degrees. On the gun the swimmer's arms move immediately forwards, and when the body is almost horizontal and the legs bent to 90 degrees the push-off from the block takes place. Some swimmers prefer to have the knees bent a little more than 120 degrees during the stance and to be rocked back a little, taking the weight of the body on the heels and controlling the rock back with the hands.

Grab start

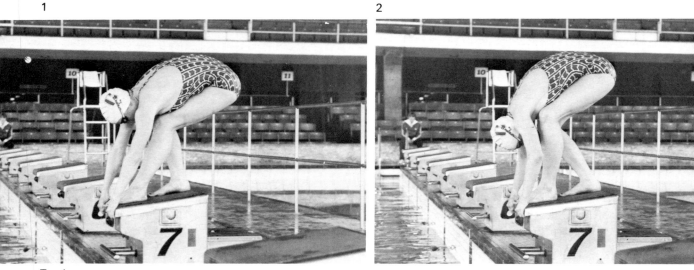

1 2

Track start

The former method seems to be the one preferred by most swimmers, however.
A recent development of this grab start has been a change in the position of the feet so that it resembles the athletic start and consequently known as the *'track start'*. The rock-back technique is employed again in this start. The toes of the front foot again grip the front of the

4

block and this leg is bent to about 120 degrees at the knee. The toes of the back foot are about 4–5 in (100–125 mm)

behind the heels of the front foot and only the ball of the foot is in contact with the block. The rear leg is bent at

90 degrees or so. In this start the hands again grip the front of the block and nearly always outside the feet.

1

2

3

Swing start

The previously 'conventional' start is known as the 'swing start'. This involves the swimmer gripping the front of the block with the toes, bending the knees to about 120 degrees again and looking forwards and downwards with the head following the natural curve of the spine. The arms are held in front of the body with the inside of the forearms either level with the ears or somewhat lower than them. On the gun as the body moves forwards in overbalancing, so the arms are swung round and backwards. As the body approaches the horizontal with the legs bent at 90 degrees so the arms are moving forwards again, which assists in pressing the feet into the block for the thrust which takes place.

The advantage of the grab and track starts lie in the fact that they give a very speedy getaway from the block which is always an advantage particularly to swimmers with slow reactions. The disadvantage with these two starts is that the momentum of the arms cannot be used to aid the start.

The swing start has the opposite advantage in that it makes full use of the arms for improving the start but is a

4

5

6

slower start in terms of time elapsed from gun to leaving the block.

The excellent grab starter should, therefore, get away from the block faster than the excellent swing starter but would be 'caught up', probably under water, as a result of the superior thrust gained from the arm swing in the start employing this.

When indicated to do so, the swimmers step up on to the back of the block. On the command 'Take your Marks' the swimmers must move forwards and downwards immediately. Any swimmer delaying taking up his starting position may be warned or disqualified by the starter. Two false starts only are permitted. The third start

actually starts the race whatever takes place before the gun is fired. Any swimmer starting before the gun is fired on the third occasion is automatically disqualified but the start does take place. If, therefore, the swimmer in Lane 1 makes two false starts and on the third makes a good start any other swimmer going before the gun, even for the first time, is disqualified.

Backstroke start

In backstroke races the start is made in the water. The hands hold the bar or grips attached to the starting block, and the feet, with the foot of the stronger leg normally 3 or 4 in (75 or 100 mm) lower than the other with the toes below the surface, are placed on the wall. The legs are bent at about 90 degrees which gives the most efficient pushing position.

The arms are flexed slightly, normally to about 120 degrees and the head is bent forwards, looking at the wall with neck following the natural curve of the spine.

On the gun the legs begin their thrust as the arms are swung backwards with the head to provide a streamlined entry once the kind of back-dive has been performed. The aim should be to clear the water with the hips; the body back will be arched in the thrust from the wall. Several leg kicks will be necessary to bring the backstroker to the surface again.

The same three start principles as in the other strokes apply in backstroke races.

Zoltan Verraszto (Hungary), showing superb elevation in his start

Turning

Many races are won and lost at the turn. Most swimmers have the necessary skill and have mastered the techniques of the various turns required by the four swimming strokes and the individual medley but few really practise them with the same quality that they apply to repetition training. If the turn is to be executed efficiently and quickly in competition, every turn performed in training must be done well. One of the most distressing aspects of the training session is to see swimmers either turning sloppily, and often illegally, or, for that matter, turning short of the wall and even at times standing up! This obviously indicates a lapse in con-centration at what to the swimmer might appear to be a relatively unimportant part of the swim being completed, but is in fact a crucial part of it. This practice also makes a mockery of repetition times. In a ninety-minute training session, in a 25 m pool, where an average 5000 m will be covered, some 199 turns must be executed and, done well each time, there should not be a great need for turning practice sessions or parts of sessions. Turns should only be practised under pressure once the turn itself has been mastered. Any swimmer can perform the turn swimming slowly into the wall when perfectly fresh. That is not what is put to the test in the race when the swimmer is under intense pressure, is suffering from the effects of fatigue and then has to execute the turn. This situation should be prevalent in every training session.

It is often said that swimming in 'chain' fashion (see 'Training Details', page 82) is detrimental to turning efficiently. The fact of the matter is that the swimmer approaches the wall as in the race but might have to push off across the lane if he or she is being closely followed. The turn itself can and should be done perfectly, and good swimmers who follow this procedure have no difficulty in competition. If turning practice is required as a group or sub-group activity during the session it should mirror as closely as possible the race situation. The swimmers should be lined up across the pool in stroke order, i.e., say a wave of backstrokers followed by a wave of butterfliers, etc. A good practice is to demand that the swimmers line up in the prone position some 7–8 m

Andreas Hargitay (Hungary), former world record-holder in the 400 m individual medley, executing a butterfly turn

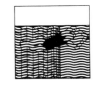

from the end. The race is from this point and back to it, which is really a test of turning ability. The first wave of swimmers should swim up one side of the lane and as soon as they leave the wall the next wave should begin to swim up the clear side of the lane. If both ends are used then a great many turns can be performed in a fifteen- to twenty-minute period. Backstroke flags should be installed for this practice. Often swimmers are undecided which turn to employ in competition and the only real test is to time the swimmer under pressure, which means a close rival in the next lane. The time starts when the swimmer's head touches a line 5 ft (1.5 m) from the turn and stops when the swimmer's head touches a line 20 ft (6 m) from the turn. This reading indicates what the turning time is. For real accuracy it is best if the swimmer swims in the lane closest to the wall. Two canes are projected over the lane, one at 5 ft (1.5 m) and the other at 20 ft (6 m). The coach stands over the 5 ft (1.5 m) marker and starts his watch as the swimmer's head is level with the cane; he then quickly moves to the 20 ft (6 m) marker and stops the watch when the swimmer's head reaches that point. When it has been decided which turn is to be used in competition it is important that the quality and speed of the turn is again checked, preferably during a relatively unimportant competition.

Every turn can be broken down into the following ways: (1) approach speed, which should be as fast as possible with as little interference with race strokes as possible; (2) the turn itself, which should be fast, efficient and reliable, meaning that it will always be done well no matter what the circumstances and will always guarantee a good foot position on the wall; (3) the push-off, which is probably the most important aspect of the turn. Most swimmers turn within a tenth of a second of each other but some push off the wall up to 2 or 3 ft (0.6 or 0.9 m) further when using the same turn. This is due partly to timing the turn better and partly to leg strength. The final aspect (4) is stroke pick-up, which has to be timed perfectly if the maximum effect is to be gained. If the swimmer breaks the streamlined push-off glide position too soon then a slowing down will occur. The opposite fault is to hold the glide too long and consequently slow down again. Stroking should commence when push-off speed reduces to maximum swimming speed. This will vary from stroke to stroke as will all the aspects. The most effective turns employed by the world's most successful swimmers include:

British international, Liz Taylor, demonstrating the butterfly turn

1

2

Butterfly

The only turn used during this stroke is almost the only one possible within the letters of the law. The swimmer is able to approach the wall without any loss of speed whatsoever. The touch is made with the arms at the end of their recovery phase, stretched out in front. The touch can be made either on, over or under the

4

water line but must be made with both hands touching simultaneously and at the same level. In most competition pools which have electronic starting pads installed, the turning walls are perfectly flat and require the touch to be made with the flat of the hand with the wrist fully extended and fingers pointing up. At the moment of touch the head should be down and the legs should 'kick' the body into the turn. As this kick is made and

5

6

almost as soon as the touch is performed, the elbows are flexed to about 90 degrees. The head then leads the turning movement of the body as one shoulder dips and the opposite arm is brought over the water and round while the other arm assists this rotation under the water. As the 'over the water' recovering arm enters the water so the head is again lowered into the water, and with both arms now beginning to straighten, the push-off is made. Throughout this turning action the legs are kept flexed with the thighs close to the chest. As the upper body moves away from the wall before the push-off occurs, it does so sufficiently to put the angle at the knee to somewhere between 90

7

8

degrees and 120 degrees—the ideal pushing position. After push-off only one or two kicks are normally necessary under water before the first arm pull comes in. The most crucial factor in the turn is the speed at which the head rotates immediately the touch is made. This will dictate the speed of the turn.

The most usual cause for disqualification is when the swimmer is found to be short of the wall but too close to put in another full stroke. This results in a small pull being made under the water which, unless followed by an over-water recovery, is illegal. If this position is encountered the swimmer must keep the hands together and kick into the wall.

1

2

Breast Stroke

The breast stroke and butterfly turns are very similar. Again, without any break in speed or stroke, the wall is met with both hands at the same time and level. The touch again will be made with the flat of the palms, wrists fully extended and fingers pointing up. Until the touch is made, below, on or slightly about the water level, the body must remain

4

perfectly flat. Most dis-
qualifications on this turn
are a result of dipping a
shoulder before the touch is
made. Exactly the same action

takes place as described in the
butterfly turn, from touch until
after push-off. The breaststroker
is allowed one complete stroke

under water after the start and
each turn. After the push-off
the body is held about 1 ft 6 in
to 2 ft (450—600 mm) below
the surface in an outstretched,

5

6

streamlined position. Once push-off speed falls off the stroke under water begins with a very strong, long-arm pull and push. Some swimmers prefer to have their arms straight and pull slightly out to the side on this, others bend their arms keeping their thumbs close to the body. In both cases the pull will not resemble the pull as used in the full racing stroke. Because of the

7

8

advantageous low-resistance circumstance of being under water the very best use must be made of the one kick and one pull allowed under water.

Once this pull has been completed another glide takes place with the body again in a streamlined

position—hands to the side, head down and toes pointed. When the speed of this glide decreases the heels are brought up to the seat and the hands

9

10

begin to recover close to the chest. As the kick is made the arms complete their recovery, the head remains down and the body again takes up its long streamlined position. It is *vital* that before the hands begin their second pull the head breaks the surface. Another common cause for disqualification is beginning the second pull before completely surfacing.

British 100 m record-holder, Joy Beasley, executing a backstroke turn

2

Backstroke

The turn employed by backstrokers is an obvious advantageous progression from the elementary 'spin turn'. The only difference between the two is that in the spin turn the turn itself is completed with the knees and lower legs in the water, whereas in the competitive turn the lower legs are brought clear of the water to cut down resistance. After a fast approach the touch is made about 12 in (300 mm) below the water line with one arm perfectly straight. This position can easily be reached if the backstroke indicator flags

3

4

situated over the water 5 m from the turn are used as markers. The touch should be made with the flat of the hand and the fingers pointing downwards. It is important that until contact with the wall is made the body remains on the back as the rules require. As the palm touches the wall so the elbows immediately flex, bringing the upper arm close to the chest and the head down into the water over that shoulder. This has the effect of bringing the lower legs out of the water, knees bent and over that side of the body which is opposite to that of the hand

6

making contact with the wall. The other hand assists, working close to the body under water, to complete the turning movement. The push-off is made with both arms above the head and they straighten completely to give a long streamlined glide position as the feet leave the wall. Again it is important that the turn allows the legs to take up a position of 90–120 degrees of knee flexion for the best possible push. When the glide speed drops, the legs are brought in to kick the body to the surface as normal stroking begins.

Lindsay Heggie, British 800 m swimmer, performing the front tumble turn

1

2

Freestyle

The turn used in freestyle races is known as the 'tumble turn'. Although essentially the same action is present it does vary according to the size of the swimmer and the distance of the race. In the sprints, because the approach speed is greater, the preliminary movements of the turn commence that much sooner. With world-class sprinters the first movement outside the normal stroking is a lowering of the head at about 2–2.5 m from the wall. This is followed by a piking at the hips as both arms are brought to the side of the body to assist with the forward

4

omersault and quarter twist which follows. During the orward somersault part of this movement, the legs are brought over the water with the legs flexed at about 90 degrees at the knees. The whole rotation takes place at a point about 1–1.5 m from the wall, and immediately the feet meet the wall, one lower than the other, both pointing to the side, the push-off is made. This is possible because the legs have recovered in this flexed efficient push position. Because in sprinting push-off speed is not too much faster than swimming speed, not too much of a glide follows. The legs are then brought in to surface the

5

6

swimmer to commence normal stroking. The push-off is made slightly on the side and the prone position is regained as the wall is left.
In distance freestyle events the swimmer needs to get much closer to the wall and needs a more efficient and less energy-consuming turn. The turn is consequently made closer to the wall and instead of the body being piked at the hips and flexed to 90 degrees at the knees, it is put into more of a tucked-up position, this being possible because it is closer to the wall. All other movements are similar to the sprint tumble turn.

Individual Medley

The laws of this race demand that the turn allowed by the stroke just completed be performed. Stroke laws cease to be applicable once the touch has been made. The butterfly to backstroke turn is quite a straightforward matter and the only problems encountered are with inexperienced swimmers who tend almost to heave themselves out of the pool on this turn. The touch should be made as for the butterfly turn. The knees are then brought up to the chest as the feet are placed on the wall. While this is taking place the arms are thrown over together above the head which is held back and between them as the push-off is made. Backstroke commences as described, following the backstroke turn. The backstroke to breast stroke turn can be performed in two ways. Both have their strengths and weaknesses. The easiest of the two is known as the 'pull-up' turn. The wall is approached at sprint speed without a break in stroking and the touch is made with the flat of the hand, fingers pointing sideways and the arm straight. The chest is then moved forwards in a rocking movement which rotates the legs under the body and allows the feet to meet the wall for the push to take place. A breath can be taken during the turn and the stroke allowed under water in breast stroke must be performed. The strength of the turn lies in the fact that a breath can be taken on the turn and in that the turn is not demanding in itself. Its disadvantage is that it tends to be done sloppily and slowly. There is also a great tendency for the backstroker to leave the position on the back when making the touch and thus bring about disqualification. The second turn is known as the 'back somersault' turn. A similar approach is made to the turn but the touching hand does so with the fingers pointing down to the bottom of the pool. The other hand quickly takes up a similar position on the wall. The head is thrust backwards, the knees brought up to the chest and a back somersault performed. This allows the feet to take up their position on the wall. The push-off is again followed by the breast-stroke pull and kick under the water. The advantage of the turn is that it is extremely fast, but it is energy-consuming and requires the breath to be held for a long time which often affects the breast-stroke pull and kick done under water. Indeed many swimmers are so exhausted after doing this turn that they do not use the stroke under water at all.

Good, efficient turns are essential for effective swimming. They should be perfected in training and executed well during the pressure and, indeed, all other periods of the training session.

Relay Take-Overs

The Law relating to relay take-overs is very simple and straightforward. It states that the swimmer 'taking over' must still be in contact with the starting block or wall as the incoming swimmer touches the end wall. The 'perfect' start, therefore, sees the swimmer that is taking off in a horizontal position but still in contact with the block or wall as the incoming swimmer touches the end with fully outstretched arms and fingers.

Obviously it takes a great deal of skill and practice to perfect such a start and it is therefore essential that the relay order is known well in advance of the competition so that practice can take place accordingly. When practice is taking place it is important that the swimmers try to mirror the conditions that are likely to prevail when the race is in progress. The incoming swimmer should be travelling at about the speed that he or she is likely to be recording at the end of their particular lap and the swimmer taking over should be well used to this speed and be able to read the take-over accordingly. The incoming swimmer should also work at adjusting the final few strokes so that the last one is made with a fully outstretched arm and fingers as opposed to the wall looming up when the arm or arms are only half recovered, or, even worse, misjudging it so badly that the final touch is almost made with the teeth! The most difficult strokes to perfect a good finish with are backstroke and butterfly. The backstroker must make full use of the overhead flags which are situated 5 m from the end, and the butterflier must adjust the final strokes so that the wall is met as the hands enter the water at the end of the recovery. It is a relatively simple matter for the freestyler and the breaststroker to make the final stroke alterations to effect a good outstretched finish.

If the lane number is known it is also important that practice takes place in that lane during the warm-up in order that the necessary familiarisation takes place. Unfortunately hours and hours of practice in one pool in one lane taking over from one particular block, will appear useless if a strange pool, lane and block are then encountered. The incoming swimmer must get used to the particular pool markings whether they be on the side or ceiling for the backstroker or on the floor of the pool for the breaststroker or freestyler. Deck-level pools offer another set of siting-the-finish problems which again will have to be solved by the incoming swimmers. The backstroker, as already mentioned, will be aided by the ceiling and backstroke flags, while the freestyler must make full use of the pool bottom markings. Most pools have marks to indicate 4 m and 2 m from the wall. These are used for water polo and are a great help to the freestyler in particular, whose head is either face down in the water or turned to the side when breathing is taking place. The breaststroker and butterflier will also be aided by these lines but can also view the finish wall as they breathe to the front.

Both the incoming swimmer and the swimmer taking over then have their own jobs to do and their own responsibilities. The swimmer making the take-over must have every confidence in, and knowledge about, the incoming swimmer because his or her movement from the block will begin when the incoming swimmer is some 2 m or so away from the wall and the start is then irrevocably executed. If the incoming swimmer judges the finish badly then obviously disqualification will result. The coach must observe the race take-overs very carefully in order to analyse exactly where the blame lies if this should happen. Often when it appears that the take-over swimmer has 'gone early' it is the fault of the incoming swimmer misjudging the finish.

The order of swimming the team depends upon various factors. In the freestyle relay the number one swimmer should be the best starter 'from the gun' in the team and should also be either the fastest or second fastest team member. It is important that the team is in front at all times if possible — this gives the swimmers much smoother water and faster times. The lead swimmer should also have an excellent finish. Number two should have good take-over and finish qualities, as should number three. Number four obviously has to finish the race off and therefore should be the fastest or second fastest in the team, depending on the other factors already mentioned. Number four should have excellent take-over ability and be used to handling the pressure of representing the team during the final high-pressure leg. Some swimmers are notoriously bad at taking over and put the team in jeopardy. In this case the swimmer in question should lead off the team. Some coaches prefer to swim their team 'from the front'; this method sees the fastest swimmer going first, the second fastest second, third fastest third, and the slowest team member last. One of the advantages of this order is that a great deal of pressure is put on to the slower swimmers who take over, hopefully in the lead and have good smooth water to race in as opposed to going in level with seven others, or even behind seven others, and having to do battle with choppy water. This is often used as a surprise tactic and will defeat many inexperienced teams who will be put off by the early lead of the opposition. If this order is employed the first two swimmers really must record good times without the pressure they would normally experience during the latter part of the relay.

The more conventional way is to swim the second fastest as number one, the third fastest number two, slowest number three, and the fastest number four. Again, however, the starting, taking-over and finishing abilities of the team members must be taken into account before finally deciding on the order.

In the medley relay the order will be pre-determined. The order of swimming is backstroke, breast stroke, butterfly, freestyle. In the medley relay, freestyle is defined as being any stroke other than those already performed, which really means that the fourth swimmer must swim front crawl, as opposed to old English backstroke or trudgen! Often the team cannot be selected until the individual events of the meet serve to act as selection trials for the team, should they come before the team race. The best team is that selected close to the event in full knowledge of the state of fitness and ability of each team member at that time. Other important knowledge is which swimmers are good relay team members. Some swimmers will only ever swim for themselves whereas others will almost die for their team! The technique of taking over from an incoming swimmer varies widely but its effectiveness will always be a result of the knowledge that the swimmer taking over has of the swimmer coming in, and the timing ability of the swimmer taking over. One method regulating 'when to go' is the sighting technique. As the incoming swimmer enters the 4 m area the take-over swimmer holds his arms together and outstretched and views the head of the incoming swimmer over the top of his hands. As the incoming swimmer's head reaches a certain siting point the start takes place. This point is usually around the 2 m mark. Some swimmers prefer to follow the head of the incoming swimmer with the arms and hands being lowered in this way from about 6 m out; this helps to indicate the speed of the incoming swimmer and leads to a most effective take-over. Other swimmers have the great ability to time the take-over from a static position. In the siting method the swing start is used while in the static start a grab or track start can be employed. Team races are often decided on take-over ability which if not practised, will certainly not be effective. Coach and swimmers must be well aware of this and must work hard if important races are to be contested.

The Strokes

Nancy Garapick (Canada), former world record-holder, 200 m backstroke

1

2

3

4

The strokes recognised by FINA for racing purposes are *backstroke*, *breast stroke*, *butterfly* and *freestyle*. In freestyle races any stroke may be swum, as the name implies, but in fact the stroke known commonly as the *front crawl* is normally performed. All the strokes are put together in the Individual Medley event.

Backstroke

Any combination of arm and leg movements may be applied in this race as long as the swimmer 'stays in the normal position on the back'. In fact an alternate arm and leg action known as the back crawl is normally performed. The photographs show the technique applied as follows:

1. The body is kept as flat as possible at all times. There will be some degree of rotation about the longitudinal axis as the shoulder of the pulling arm dips so as to allow the pectoral muscles to come into action. There is no snaking whatsoever. **2.** The arms provide most of the power. As one arm pulls so

the other one recovers. There is a very slight 'catching up' that takes place during the arm action. The action can be said to begin as the hand enters the water. The way in which this entry takes place is crucial. The only way for the hand to enter the water and be rendered immediately useful for pulling

1

2

5

6

7

8

purposes is with the little finger first. If the little finger enters the water first the palm of the hand is facing directly backwards and an effective pull can be made. When the hand enters the water in this manner it then travels down for about 9–12 in (230–300 mm) at which point the backward action becomes possible. This

is known as the *'catch'* point. When the catch is made there follows an immediate bending of the arm at the elbow. This then enables the hand to apply its force directly backwards. The anatomy of the elbow and shoulder determine the exact path described by the hand as it attempts to move backwards in a straight line. In fact what

actually happens to the hand is that after the catch position as the body moves forwards so the position of the hand moves downwards in a curving manner and then similarly upwards to a curve that reaches its highest point when the hand is level with the shoulder. At this point the elbow is bent at its greatest —

1

2

3

an angle of just over 90 degrees. The palm continues to face backwards and at this point the little finger will be pointing downwards. As the shoulder moves forwards of the hand, another curving action takes place as the arm straightens; the hand curves to its deepest point somewhere close to the thigh and just below it. This final pressing down, although not contributing to propulsion, serves to lift that shoulder clear of the water, thus aiding recovery. The recovery itself is made with a straight but relaxed arm. Early rotation of the arm in order to develop the little-finger-first entry is recommended. If the little

4

finger leads the recovery throughout — that is, if it is the first part of the hand to leave the water after the pull — then this will also assist the raising of the shoulder. The hand should enter the water directly above the shoulder. If too narrow an entry is attempted a 'snaking' of the body often results. The pull itself is often referred to as the 'bent-arm' pull, and it can be seen that as the body moves past the hand so the hand describes the shape of an 'S' on its side.

3. The leg action begins at the hips and the propulsion is gained as a result of the instep and lower leg 'fixing' on the water at the lowest point of the kick so that as the leg straightens the foot moves upwards. The downwards part of the action can be regarded as almost the recovery phase. When the leg reaches the bottom of its recovery movement the knee bends and the feet will be somewhere in the region of 1 ft 6 in to 2 ft (450–600 mm) below the surface. At this point the toes are fully extended, hyper-extended if possible. As the instep and lower leg 'fix' on to

the water and apply a force in a backwards and upwards direction, so the leg straightens and the body is moved forwards. When the leg is perfectly straight the toes will just break the surface. As with the arms, when one leg kicks so the other recovers.

4. The timing of the stroke, the relationship between the movement of the arms and legs, is normally that for each complete arm cycle so the legs kick six times. Very little variation takes place with regard to this rule.

5. Breathing in backstroke presents no real problems because of the face being out of the water. However, a breathing pattern should be mastered. Most backstrokers breathe in as the same arm recovers on each cycle. For sprinting, when breath-holding might be necessary the same technique is applied. Backstroke races are held over 100 m and 200 m. The pacing of these races is discussed in 'Pace Judgement', on page 101. The backstroke 100 m World Record is only fractionally slower than the butterfly World

Record, even with the start having to be made in the water. With a dive start it would probably join the butterfly as the second fastest stroke — both some $4\frac{1}{2}$ seconds, or 9 m, slower than freestyle. During training sessions the backstrokers will have to perform arms-only practices, using pull-buoys; legs-only practices with the hands held together extended above the head in the water, and full stroke practices. The usual other stroke work and individual medley work for variety in training will also be necessary. The start and turn for the race are detailed in the chapters 'Starting' and 'Turning', on pages 27 and 37.

Of over-riding importance in this stroke is the flexibility of the shoulders and ankles. Everything possible should be done to improve this. Also vital, yet often neglected, is the condition of the legs. Backstrokers must have superbly conditioned legs if they are really going to succeed.

1  2  3

Breast Stroke

The rules of the stroke state that all movements of the arms and legs must be in a simultaneous and symmetrical manner. Movement in the vertical plane is not allowed, and this rules out the possibility of a dolphin-type kick. Also, the recovery of the arms must be made under the water. This no movement in the vertical plane, together with the need for the arms to be recovered under the water, differentiates this stroke from butterfly and has done since the formalising of the latter stroke in 1953.

Photographs show the technique applied as follows:

1. The body position does vary throughout the various phases of the stroke but an attempt should be made to keep the body as flat as possible at all times. This is particularly important during the breathing and leg recovery phases. The head must break the surface of the water at least once during every stroke with the exceptions of the single

1   2   3

 4

 5

 6

underwater strokes allowed at the start and at each turn.

2. In recent years the arms have come to play a much greater part in the propulsion of the stroke. In the past the arms were used largely for balance and for maintaining body position, in addition to providing a support for the head to be lifted. This meant

that the arm action tended to be wide, quite deep and performed with straight arms. Breast stroke today is swum with the emphasis on the arms being used for propulsion. This, along with an adjustment in the timing of breathing in the stroke, has resulted in great improvements being made. With the arms outstretched and

together in front of the head, face downwards, the arms begin their movement. Moving outwards to about 1 ft 6 in (450 mm) apart and downwards about 1 ft (350 mm), the hands, wrists flexing slightly, reach their 'catch' position. 'Fixing' on these two points, the hands exert pressure backwards and,

4

5

6

while remaining relatively still themselves, they allow the body to be pressed forwards. Because the body itself has to approach these two points of 'fix', the hands in fact move outwards while the elbows and shoulders rotate over these points. Before the elbows and shoulders are over these two points, the hands begin to describe a sculling motion which exerts further pressure backwards and inwards. The palms at this stage are in fact moving towards each other and the elbows tucking into the body so that when the sculling has ceased and maximum arm speed is reached, the arms are tucked in close to the body, making it as streamlined as possible. The recovery of the

7

arms from this tucked-in position is often completed with the palms facing slightly upwards. This assists the movement of the elbows into the body. The extension of the arms to the outstretched position should be done in as streamlined a way as possible.

3. The leg action provides the stroke with about two-thirds of its propulsion. It is also a fact that about two-thirds of this power is derived from the vital first third of the kick. The kick should begin with the heels close to the seat, feet turned outwards with the soles of the feet and inside surfaces of the lower leg facing backwards. At this point the knees will be about 9–12 in (230–300 mm) apart and the heels about 1 ft 6 in to 2 ft (450–600 mm) apart. The knees should not be too far under the body. The angle between thigh and body should be in the region of 120 degrees.
If this is the case then the quadricep muscles of the thigh which straighten the lower legs and the gluteal muscles of the backside which extend the upper leg, will be in effective positions. A fair amount of

resistance will be encountered at this position, but this should not be increased any more, otherwise positive retardation will take place during each recovery of the legs. If an angle greater than 120 degrees is obtained, and it can be quite easily, resistance is reduced but the kicking muscles are in a most ineffective position which results in a very weak kick taking place. The path traced by the feet as the kick is made is a long, narrow, spherical one and is illustrated in the photographs.

4. The timing of when the breath is taken is all important in competitive breast stroke. In most physical activities, such as throwing a punch in the boxing ring, or heading a soccer ball, it is important to hold the breath when the effort of punching or heading is taking place. The same principle applies in swimming. When the pull is taking place the breath should be held. The head is lifted at the end of the pull and the breath is taken during the main propulsive phase. There are many advantages in doing this. They include:

(i) if the head is down during the pull the feet will be up, the body in a streamlined position, thus rendering the arms able to pull more effectively;

(ii) with the face in the water the air in the lungs makes the body more buoyant which again improves the body position;

(iii) when the lungs are full of air and the breath is being held, the rib cage becomes very firm. This provides the pulling muscles, the pectorals and the latissimus dorsi, with a firm base from which to act;

(iv) finally, if the head is down and the body in this buoyant, streamlined position, the swimmer is more likely to appreciate this and use the hands and forearms to apply a force backwards instead of perhaps pressing downwards to lift the head in order that a breath can be taken.

rms were meant for pulling
ot breathing! The type of
reath varies depending on
whether sprint breast stroke or
00 m breast stroke is being
wum. Swimmers rarely have to
e told *how* to breathe. As long
s they master the timing they
hould not experience any
roblems.

he photographs illustrate just
ow the kick fits in with the
ull. The world's best
reaststrokers employ a short
lide after the kick before the
ext pull begins. This is
ecause most breaststrokers
an kick faster than they can
ull and consequently they
wait until the kick speed has
dropped to pull speed before
ringing the arms in again.
Very simply speaking, the legs
ecover as the arms pull and
vice versa. Breathing normally
akes place on each stroke.
Breast-stroke races are held
over 100 m and 200 m. During
raining for this stroke a lot of
eg work will be necessary
because of the important part
hat they play in the stroke.
One word of warning, however,
elates to the possible danger
of putting too much pressure
on the knee joint. It is
mperative that breaststrokers

Debbie Rudd (City of Coventry Swimming Club and Great Britain), coached by the author. Finalist in 200 m breast stroke, 1976 Montreal Olympics, and Commonwealth 200 m record-holder

warm up correctly before
getting into any really hard
kicking drills. This warm-up
can be performed both on
land with the use of simple
squatting practices and in the
water by beginning kicking
very slowly and increasing the
pressure gradually. Once
damage to the knee has taken
place it can recur with
frustrating regularity at
important times. Legs-only
practices should be done
with a kickboard, although
to prevent any cheating
whatsoever, a good practice is
to have the breaststrokers do
legs-only with the hands held
together behind the back.

Arms-only can be a useful
practice, although if it is not
well controlled this can easily
become a butterfly legs-only
practice. Pull-buoys are
essential if this practice is to be
done well.

The breaststrokers will have to
employ both freestyle and
individual medley work in their
schedules and will not normally
swim much over 400 m breast
stroke. Most repetition work
will be done over 50 m, 100 m
and 200 m.

The correct timing of the stroke
is vital and should be considered carefully by swimmer
and coach at all times.

Butterfly

FINA law states that the swimmer must remain on the front at all times and that all movements should be made simultaneously. Recovery of the arms must take place over the water. As mentioned earlier, the stroke is similar in speed to the backstroke, the two strokes having similar records at Olympic and World levels. Butterfly became a stroke in its own right in 1953 following the Helsinki Olympic Games of 1952 when most of the breaststrokers used an over-arm recovery — butterfly breast stroke. It is still considered to be the hardest and most strenuous of the strokes. The fact of the matter is that it is the stroke that is swum and practised the least. At the lower level it is not an easy stroke to master and until it is properly mastered it is a very strenuous one. However, later on when a good style has been acquired, it becomes little more difficult than the other strokes. Unfortunately swimmers not too proficient will appeal to the coach, and more as a result of pity than logic and understanding the coach will make various dispensations for the butterflier that will result in less butterfly being done!

Butterfly

1

2

Again the stroke can be broken down into the phases of:

1. The body position should remain as flat as possible throughout the stroke. Butterfly used to be called the 'dolphin'. Unfortunately this conjures up an illusion of the butterflier having to dive to the bottom of the pool and then dive completely out of it during each stroke! Nothing could be further from the truth. The butterflier should use the body to effect a good arm stroke and leg kick. It must be kept as flat as possible to reduce resistance but will have to undulate somewhat in order to facilitate the arm pull and leg kick. The hips should keep close to the surface throughout the stroke.

2. The arms provide the bulk of the propulsion. As in freestyle, the hands should enter in order of fingers, wrists and then elbows, somewhere between the centre line and the shoulders, in front of the body. Many swimmers enter thumbs first which tends to encourage a pressing action out to the side. What is required is a pressure downwards and backwards. Telling the swimmers to attempt to enter with the fingers down and slightly turned inwards will help. As the hands travel down about 1 ft (300 mm) below the surface, so the 'catch' is made. The arms are almost straight at this point. A backwards pressure is then applied and, as the hands 'fix' in the water, so the body is levered forwards. In order that the body can be pressed towards and then past the hands, and because the arms are in a position that is uneconomical to exert a major force during the early part of the pull, they tend to move out to the side until the shoulders come level with the hands which are then at their widest.

71

3 4

because of the facts just stated. The recovery of the arms is largely a matter of choice although normally dictated by flexibility of the shoulders. World records have been broken by using a bent-arm recovery as well as a straight-arm recovery.

3. The leg kick is initiated at the hips and the fluid movement travels down to the toes. At the top of the kick, with the toes hyper-extended if possible so that they point upwards and backwards, the knees bend to an angle of approximately 120–150 degrees, and on the downward kick, propulsion is gained. This bending of the knees allows the insteps and front surfaces of the lower legs to be pointing backwards. These surfaces again fix on the water. As the legs kick so they straighten and move the body forwards. On the up-kick there is only a very small force exerted backwards and this aspect of the kick can be assumed to be the recovery phase. The flexibility of the ankles is vital in that the feet should be in almost a vertical position as the down-kick begins. Either a single or a

The elbows should be bent to about 90 degrees at this point. After the shoulders have moved past the hands so the pull becomes narrow again as the hands come close to the body during the later stages of the pull. Then, at the very end of the pull, which is in fact the push phase, the hands move

outwards again in order to avoid the body and assist the recovery of the arms. Viewed from underneath the swimmer, this pull pattern would give the appearance of a keyhole; the pull is often referred to as this. Swimmers, however, should be told simply to press backwards and the correct pull will result

Note insteps and front surfaces of lower legs applying force backwards and downwards during down beat

double kick can be applied in the full stroke. If a single kick is employed then this tends to take place as the hands enter the water. The reason for this is that at this point the body is moving through the water at its slowest and the kick enables this speed to be at least maintained or improved upon if the butterflier has a good, effective kick. If two beats are used then usually the 'major', the stronger of the two, takes place on entry and the 'minor' occurs at the end of the pull.

4. The timing of the leg action has already been discussed. The breath is taken at the highest point in the stroke which occurs as the arms are about halfway through their recovery phase.

5. Breathing can be either to the side or to the front, the most common method.

Races are over 100 m and 200 m. During training, most repetition work will be over 50 m, 100 m and 200 m, although the occasional 400 m butterfly might be included. Throughout these sessions it is important that the arms recover completely over the water. Butterfliers will also use freestyle and individual medley as a means of varying their demanding sessions. Kicking practices should be done with a large float and pulling practice with a pull-buoy.

Freestyle

In this race any stroke can be swum, but front crawl, being the fastest, is the one normally employed. The men's world record for the 100 m race represents a speed of just about 5 mph (8 km/h). In the medley relay team race and the individual medley race, this stroke 'freestyle' is further conditioned as being 'any stroke other than the ones already employed'. This further improves the case for using front crawl.

As with the other strokes, freestyle, as we will call it, can be broken down in the following way:

1. The body position should remain as flat as possible in the water. There will be a rotation of the upper body about the longitudinal axis as the head is turned to breathe and as the roll occurs to enable a more efficient pull as explained in the:

2. Arm action: the 'jet engines', so to speak, of the

1

2

3

Freestyle

freestyler, are the arms. The vast majority of the propulsion comes from the arm action, although at one point in the stroke, when the push has just been completed with one hand and the catch not quite established with the other, there occurs a dead spot. At this point the leg kick does probably aid propulsion,

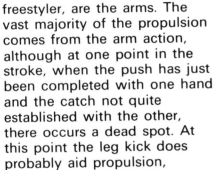

especially in the sprint events. The arm enters the water in front of the body somewhere between the centre line of the body and the shoulder line. The elbow should be high at this point as the fingers, wrist then elbow enter the water. The catch is made at about 1 ft (300 mm) below the surface and the downwards and backwards force is applied. As the hand and forearm fix on the water, so the body is pressed past that point. The elbow bends sufficiently to allow the palm to face backwards throughout this action and is at approximately 90 degrees when the shoulder is over the hand. Because the shoulder has passed the hand, the latter part of the action is often referred to as the push phase. The fingers should be

about ¼ in (6 mm) apart for the best results to be made on the water and the hand should be flat, *not* cupped in any way! The degree of arm bend, as discussed in the chapter on mechanics, will depend upon the strength of the swimmer and the length of the race. The recovery is made again with the elbow 'high'. This ensures a good entry and catch and is also the quickest method of recovery. There are many very successful swimmers, however, who employ other styles of recovery. If the swimmer prefers a certain method and it is not interfering with the vitally important aspect of propulsion, or the body position, then it may be left alone. A straight swinging arm recovery, for instance, tends to set up a swaying of the body and the legs, which is obviously detrimental to performance. This recovery would have to be adjusted.

3. The leg action is quite a simple one and a similar one to that employed in the backstroke but more shallow. At the top of the kick (see photographs at the top of page 74), with the toes just on the water surface,

4

the ankles hyper-extended again, the knee bends to about 150 degrees. This enables the instep and lower leg front surface to be facing backwards. With the toes now pointing almost vertically the instep fixes on the water, and as pressure is applied backwards and downwards, so the foot remains relatively still and the leg straightens, moving the body forwards. Propulsion is therefore gained from the down-kick of the action and the up-kick can be regarded as the recovery phase. It obviously helps to have large, wide feet and good ankle extension. The kick itself will vary with the event. The kicking muscles, the quadriceps and gluteals, are extremely large and rapid-energy-using muscle groups. In the sprints, where every bit of propulsion has to be called in,

a six-beat strong leg action is used. In the distances, where conservation of energy is an important factor, a two- or four-beat action is employed. This kick serves to provide a balance to the stroke and maintains the all-important flat body position.

4. The timing of the stroke then depends upon the length of the race. The sprints require six leg kicks to each arm cycle, while in the distance events either two or four kicks per arm cycle are performed.

5. Breathing takes place to the recovering arm side and begins as the catch position is reached. Bilateral breathing is, as the name suggests, when breathing takes place to alternate sides, normally on every third arm pull. In sprint

freestyle breath-holding is employed. This usually takes the form of the breath being held for the first 15 m to 20 m and then the breath being taken every three or six arm cycles.

Freestyles use a lot of arms-only and legs-only practices in their training programmes. Repetitions range from 25 m to 3000 m in length although the bulk of them tend to be at 50 m, 100 m, 200 m and 400 m. Freestyle is the most frequently used stroke in training because by using it more distance can be covered in a given time than with any other stroke. It is used as a conditioner for swimmers irrespective of what their race stroke might be. Races are held internationally from 100 m through to 800 m for women and 1500 m for men.

The Individual Medley

The order of swimming the four strokes in the individual medley race is butterfly, backstroke, breast stroke and freestyle, which must be any stroke other than those already completed. The appropriate turn for the stroke just completed is called for and has been discussed in the chapter, 'Turning', which starts on page 37.

The strokes performed are identical to the strokes already discussed although conditioned somewhat by the demands of the event. The individual medley race takes place over 200 m and 400 m and is considered to be the most difficult one to pace. This problem is discussed in the chapter, 'Pace Judgement', on page 101.

Putting the strokes together in the individual medley often upsets the normal stroking rate of them as occurs when they are being swum individually. For instance, after the very demanding butterfly 'leg' the swimmer often begins backstroke in a much relieved frame of mind! This, allied with the fact that the butterfly is a relatively slow double-arm action, results in the backstroke leg being done with too slow an arm action. Swimmers must be coached to speed up the arm action as soon as they pick up backstroke from the turn. Butterfly and backstroke are both arm-dominant strokes and consequently when the breast-stroke section is reached this, tending to be a leg-dominant stroke, provides a little rest for the arms. During this phase of the event, because it lasts the longest, great deficits can be retrieved and great leads established by an individual medley swimmer with a good breast-stroke leg action.

As the arms are slightly refreshed the freestyle section can be done efficiently, and again the early speed of the stroke is all important; because of the change from the relatively slow breast stroke the freestyler often sets off with too slow an arm action and does not really 'get going' until the race is almost over. It is quite amazing that after this extremely demanding race nearly all swimmers have 'something left' during the final stages of the freestyle leg.

Planning the Year

Most countries around the world have now adopted the 'two-season year'. This is a programme of short-course (25 m) events leading up to a national championship normally in March or April and a series of long-course (50 m) leading up to a national championship usually in August. These national championships often serve as national trials for major Games such as the European Championships, the Pan American Games, the Commonwealth Games or the Olympic Games. This is somewhat unfortunate in that trials should be held as near to the final entry deadline as possible, and should have an order of events similar to the championships or games that are to be contested. Another problem is that most countries have national club cham-

A typical year laid out as for senior swimmers

	Saturdays, Week Ending	No. weeks prior to major comp.	
August	21		
	28		Popular time for
September	4		International
	11		Fixtures and Major
	18		Games
	25		
October	2		Relatively slack period
	9		for swim meets and a
	16		good time to have a break
	23		
	30		
November	6		
	13		
	20		
	27		School Holidays
December	4		
	11		
	18		
	25		
January	1	12	
	8	11	
	15	10	
	22	9	
	29	8 ⎫	
February	5	7 ⎬	
	12	6 ⎭	
	19	5	
	26	4	

	1 2 3 4 5 6
JAN	
FEB	☒ ☒ ☒
MAR	☒
APL	
MAY	

March	5	3	
	12	2	School Holidays
	19	1	
	26		NATIONAL SHORT COURSE CHAMPIONSHIPS
April	2		Popular time for
	9		international
	16		fixtures around
	23		the world.
	30		
May	7		
	14		
	21	12	
	28	11	
June	4	10	District long course
	11	9	Championships or
	18	8	Regional.
	25	7	
July	2	6	
	9	5	
	16	4	
	23	3	School Holidays
	30	2	
August	6	1	
	13		NATIONAL LONG COURSE CHAMPIONSHIPS

pionships decided at the 'nationals', and clubs and coaches require their swimmers to compete in as many events as possible for the purpose of gaining points. This possible conflict should be prevented if at all possible, and trials ensure this.

The swimming coach will also be faced with having to prepare age-group swimmers for their own 'nationals' as well as the senior team.

In planning the year the two most important dates must be marked clearly, and the weeks before those dates numbered accordingly.

The plan shows the importance of starring the two most important dates, in this case the National Short Course Championships and the National Long Course Championships. It is most

	1	2	3	4	5	6
JAN						
FEB				■	■	
MAR	✕	✕				
APL						
MAY						

useful to number the weeks from 1 to 12 during the period immediately before these two events in order that the work for that duration can be carefully planned. Also on the plan such things as school holidays, any district and/or regional competitions and any other events that might influence the plan should be added.

It can be seen from the plan illustrated that school holidays often do coincide with the major events. This obviously assists in the swimmers not having to miss school in order to compete, and when the break precedes the event it also allows more time and often more convenient time in which to prepare.

It has been found that a 'build-up' to an important event should ideally be about ten to twelve weeks long. If the period is much longer, the event will be too distant in the minds of the swimmers and this period often only produces low interest and low-quality work. The twelve-week build-up allows for a gradual introduction to the preparation, a lead into an endurance period which is then followed by more of a quality period which is completed by the 'taper' period.

Work outside these two periods — unless the swimmer is involved in international or other representative duties — should be concerned with stroke technique, starting and turning skills, as well as with work on land to improve strength and flexibility. This serves to act as a break for the swimmer and enables a fresh, positive start to be made to the two important build-up periods. The details of the build-up appear in 'Training Details', on page 81.

Other aspects of planning the year include the selection of team officials for the particular contests who will in turn have to organise the necessary transport and accommodation.

Team officials must obviously be compatible, must have worked together and must know the swimmers and each other as well as possible. Transport is easy enough to arrange and consideration should be given to its being retained for the duration of the championships should it be necessary. The correct hotel or guest house is a vital matter; the wrong one could upset the swimmers and ruin the detailed preparation that has taken place. It should be ascertained that single beds are available for all swimmers and that preferably there are never more than two to each room. If three or four swimmers share a room the incidence of late-night chatting etc., is increased alarmingly. The correct food should be available at suitable times and such things as drying facilities for swim wear and towels should not be over-looked. These might sound relatively unimportant matters that will add up to the success or otherwise of the team at this vital time.

Training Details

Before any form of training can take place the group itself must be selected. There are many ways of doing this and many factors must be taken into consideration when selecting the swimmers.

Most groups work towards two main targets each year, as discussed in the chapter, 'Planning the Year', on page 78. It is therefore preferable that all members are working towards the same goal. This means that they should be of similar competitive ability. If this is the case it will make the coach's job much easier. It also helps if the group are all of a reasonably similar training ability. The problem here is that the whole group can be held up by one poor trainer. Age is another factor that has to be considered.

Obviously the coach will know what training times he wishes to operate, how many early-morning sessions he wishes to include, etc. The swimmers, having been selected for the group by whatever method used, will also have to accept the 'Rules' of the group.

One of the best methods of selecting a group is to select from an ability band of a scale of times. These might be local, county, district or national times. It could be that to make the top group in the club that you had to achieve a time within ten seconds of the national age group qualifying time for your age, in your best stroke at your best distance. In order to make the second group this time might be between twenty and eleven seconds outside the qualifying times, and so on. This ensures an equal-ability group and after the other conditions that we have mentioned have been checked there can be no grumbles about the group composition – but there probably will be! The advantage of this method is that the swimmers know exactly what they have to do to get promotion and what they must not do if they wish to avoid demotion! Regular trials are a big help in keeping the groups competitive.

The coach will check such things as punctuality, attendance and effort, and when the new groups are being considered these factors should be taken into account. It is usual that as a swimmer improves so he is offered a place in a higher group which will mean more sessions, possibly more early-morning sessions, harder training and

Chain swimming

often higher fees. If the offer is accepted it is assumed by the coach that the swimmer accepts all the conditions of the group.

Once the groups have been formed training can begin. The coach will have planned the year and should explain it in some detail to both parents and swimmers. This will put them fully in the picture as to what the requirements and the targets for the year are. The coach will explain the group timetable for both training and competition.

When training begins the coach will allocate swimmers to various lanes. In swimming, Lane 1 is always on the right facing the course. One lane allocation will be for first-choice strokes. Here the breaststrokers will move into one lane, the backstrokers into another and so on. For other pieces of work, such as distance freestyle, the coach may well have training ability lanes so that the best trainers on a particular piece of work will do that work in the same lane.

When swimming in lanes, two methods are employed. The first method is used for distance work or a number of repetitions of more than, say, two lengths. This method is known as **chain swimming**. Normally the swimmers in odd-numbered lanes swim in a clockwise fashion, that is, up the left-hand side of the lane and down the right-hand side. Swimmers in even-numbered lanes swim in an anticlockwise direction. The centre of the lane is used only for any

Wave swimming

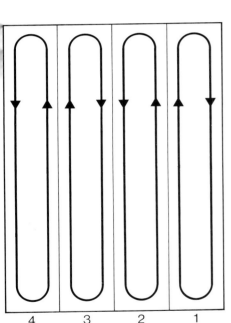

4   3   2   1

Chain swimming

overtaking that might be
necessary. The reason for using
this directional method is that
whenever two swimmers are on
opposite sides of the lane line

they are swimming in the same
direction. This minimises the
effect of injury resulting from
any collisions that occur. When
using this method it is best to
have swimmers of similar
training speed together in each
lane, irrespective of stroke. This
will mean that the minimum
amount of overtaking will be
necessary. Chain swimming can
and is used, however, when

first-choice strokes are being
used in the programme, each
stroke taking up one lane. As
mentioned earlier chain
swimming is chiefly used for
the many repetitions, longer
repetitions and distance work
that will be necessary to
improve endurance.

The second method is known
as the **wave system**. Here the
fastest swimmers are spread

out across the pool and the race is simulated. This is used for short, fast repetition work under highly competitive conditions and is aimed at increasing the sprinting quality of the swimmers. The freestyle sprinters would usually be in the first 'wave' and the breaststrokers usually in the last wave. Only short repetitions can be used in this method because of the catching up that will naturally occur.

In both systems swimmers using the training clock, as explained earlier, would begin their repeats five or ten seconds after the swimmer in front.

There are many types of work that the coach can select from and it is this selection and combination that will bring about success or failure. Some of the work available to the coach includes the four strokes, individual medley, arms only, legs only, certain stroke drills, pace work, broken swims (a method of breaking one of the sprints down into say 4×25 m with ten seconds rest and timing the actual swimming time), and other high-quality work, starting, turning, finishing and relay take-overs.

In the out-of-season periods and early in the two build-up periods the work will tend to stress stroke technique and endurance; this might be for a freestyler say 4×800 m freestyle every twelve minutes aiming for eleven minutes. Here the number and distance of the repeat has been stated as has the stroke, the resting interval (every twelve minutes means that if the swimmer records a time of ten minutes he has two minutes rest but if the time recorded is eleven minutes thirty seconds then the resting interval is cut to thirty seconds), and the target time. All these aspects of the swim will be set by the coach. As the swimmer gets fitter so the number of repetitions will increase, the resting period be reduced and the target time improved. Later on in the preparation the number and distance of repetitions is reduced and the resting interval increased which should bring about much faster swimming times. The swimmer who began the build-up twelve weeks before his major competition of the year with 4×800 m on twelve minutes aiming for eleven minutes might be doing 6×800 m on 11½ minutes aiming for 10½ minutes after four weeks and 3×800 m on thirteen minutes aiming for ten minutes after eight weeks. This illustrates how the number of repetitions goes up as the swimmer gets fitter and is then reduced when faster swimming is required.

The longer the distance and the greater the number of repetitions the more will endurance only be gained. A shorter distance and fewer repetitions will result in more speed being gained. The swimmer requires both of these qualities and it will be up to the coach to know how to put all the variety of work and quality of work at his disposal together to bring about the best results. The ingredients are available but it takes a good deal of skill on the part of the coach and application on the part of the swimmer to produce a first-class swim at the correct time.

Repetitions in training can vary from 3000 m down to 25 m or less if the pool is shorter. The number of repetitions can be as many as, say, 128, although these would tend to be done in blocks of, say, sixteen or thirty-two, and as few as one or two. The rest between repetitions can be as little as three

Swimmer: Male age 14
      Best times:
            100 m free: 1.02.0
            200 m free: 2.14.0
            400 m free; 4.34.0
            800 m free: 9.25.0
            1500 m free: 17.50.0
Background: Has been used to training 7–8 sessions per week
      of 1 hour each session.
Pool Length: 25 m
Work Chart:

No. of weeks prior to major competition	Total distance to be covered each week	1500			800			400			200			100			50			25		
		N	F	T	N	F	T	N	F	T	N	F	T	N	F	T	N	F	T	N	F	T
12	28,000 m	2	24	21	4	13	11.15	8	6½	5.30	16	3¼	2.45	32	1.40	1.20	64	50	36	—	—	—
11	28,000 m	2	24	20.30	4	13	11	8	6½	5.20	16	3¼	2.40	32	1.40	1.18	64	50	36	—	—	—
10	32,000 m	3	23	20	6	12½	11	16	6	5.20	32	3	2.40	64	1.30	1.18	96	45	34	—	—	—
9	32,000 m	4	23	20	8	11½	10.45	16	6	5.15	32	3	2.35	64	1.30	1.17	96	45	34	—	—	—
8	32,000 m	4	23	20	8	11½	10.30	16	6	5.15	32	3	2.35	64	1.30	1.17	96	45	34	32	30	15
7	32,000 m	3	23	19	6	11	10.15	12	5.45	5	24	3¼	2.30	48	1.30	1.16	64	45	33	32	30	15
6	28,000 m	2	24	18.30	4	11	10	8	5.45	4.55	16	3¼	2.25	32	1.40	1.12	32	50	32	16	40	15
5	24,000 m	2	24	18.15	4	11½	9.45	8	5.30	4.50	16	3¼	2.25	32	1.40	1.10	32	50	31	16	40	15
4	20,000 m	1	—	18	2	12	9.30	4	5.45	4.45	8	3½	2.20	16	1.50	1.08	16	55	30.5	8	30	14.5
3	16,000 m	—	—	—	1	—	9.15	2	6	4.40	4	3½	2.18	8	2	1.07	8	60	30	8	50	14.5
2	16,000 m	—	—	—	—	—	—	—	—	—	4	3¼	2.16	8	2½	1.06	4	80	29	4	60	14
1	12,000 m	—	—	—	—	—	—	—	—	—	2	4	2.14	4	3	1.04	2	90	28	4	60	13.5

N = number of repetitions
F = frequency of repetitions
T = target time

seconds or as much as five minutes. The speed of the swim can be a matter of minutes outside the swimmer's personal best in the case of the 1500 m swimmer or only tenths of a second outside in the case of a sprinter at a time close to the event.

All these possibilities are probably best illustrated in chart form (see page 85) but it must be stressed that this is a very general view of the situation as it might affect one swimmer. It would also possibly be varied should the coach so desire.

From the chart the trend can be seen as detailed. The first two weeks are spent getting the swimmer back into the swing of things. The next four weeks are spent on pure endurance work getting in as many repetitions as possible at a fair pace but with as little rest as possible. Six weeks away from the competition sees the workload cut down a little, more rest introduced and consequently better times required. The final two weeks see a great reduction in the quantity of work — less than 50 per cent of what was being achieved in weeks 10, 9, 8 and 7 before competition but a corresponding increase in the quality of the work. It may well be that the swimmer has to be varied from this general pattern. Swimmers vary tremendously in what type of work suits them physiologically and psychologically. Some will be able to accept very long series of repetitions, such as 16 × 400 m, both mentally and physically. It is the job and skill of the coach to determine exactly what programme the swimmer will be asked to follow. The table gives a very approximate indication of the type of work, rest and rate that could be expected from a swimmer as outlined. Also into this programme will have to be scheduled the other varieties of training that have been discussed.

The swimmer would not be set a schedule solely from the table but his or her 'main piece' of work would come from it. Typical sessions in weeks 12, 8 and 2 might be as shown in the next column.

Week 12 (afternoon session of 2 hours)
- will aim to cover 3500 m
- warm up: 500 m backstroke/breast stroke (alternate lengths) — (10 min.)
- main piece: 2 × 800 m free on 13 mins. target 11.15 secs (26 mins.)
  3 × 400 m free on 6½ target 5 mins. 30 secs. (20 mins.)
- = 3200 m/56 mins. swimming time.

Week 8
- will aim to cover 4000 m
- warm up: 300 m backstroke
- main piece: 6 × 400 free on 6 mins. target 5.15
  6 × 200 free on 3 mins. target 2.35
- = 3900 m/59 mins. swimming time.

Week 2
- will aim to cover 2000 m
- warm up: 400 m easy (any stroke)
- main piece: 3 × 200 free on 3.45 target 2 mins. 16 secs. Rest 5 mins.
  3 × 100 free on 2.30 target 1 min. 6 secs. Rest 3 mins.
- 3 × 50 free on 1.20 target 29.0
  300 easy swim down practice starts and turns (15 mins.)
- = 1750 m in 45 mins. plus starts and turns.

different type of scale would have to be arrived at for the other strokes. It would be more than a little unkind to the butterfly swimmer if 3×1500 appeared on the programme no matter what the resting or pace was!

Into the programmes have to be placed work on other strokes for variety; individual medley work for the 'I.M. specialist' as well as more variety. Arms only, legs only, pace work and all the other aspects of training must be borne in mind by the coach when he sets his programme. Work charts similar to the one just discussed are for guidance only and the success or otherwise of the programme has to be constantly assessed by both coach and swimmer. One great advantage of such charts is that should the chief coach be absent it is very easy to assess how the programme has progressed, and another assistant coach should not have too much difficulty in carrying on the programme.

The ability to be able to do this is all-important. The group or team should not suffer unduly if the chief coach has to be absent.

Other Methods of Conditioning

The physical qualities of a swimmer could be broken down into the areas of *endurance*, *flexibility* and *strength*.

All these qualities can be improved on land as well as in the water. Indeed, strength and flexibility are easier improved on land.

As a result of hard training the swimmer will gain a lot of endurance, a good deal of flexibility but not too much strength. The hundreds and hundreds of repetitions to which the body is constantly exposed makes it adapt to these stresses, and endurance is gained. The limbs have to perform the necessary movements thousands of times during each session which improves the flexibility of the swimmer. The swimmer, especially the young distance swimmer, does not require a great deal of strength to overcome the relatively small water pressure forces, and consequently swimming itself does not bring about a substantial increase in strength. Endurance on land can be improved in several ways, such as by playing team games, running, circuit training and the use of certain resistance exercisers which can be small and portable or very large and static. Most swimmers will tend to be involved in games and physical education at schools and will benefit from the games and running aspects of this. Obviously, too much games playing and running could well prove detrimental to swimming but the ten-mile cross country run done three or four times each week is not usual in school PE programmes.

The two best ways of gaining extra endurance are via circuit training and the use of resistance exercises. These two methods are invaluable if it is difficult to get enough water time for training. Many swimmers have reached the top by training solely in the water, but they obviously had sufficient endurance, strength and flexibility to do so.

Circuit training consists of a number of exercises placed in a circuit. The swimmer moves round the circuit and attempts either to complete as many repetitions as possible at each stage in a set time or does a fixed number at each stage and gets round the circuit as quickly as possible. There are several types of circuit that can be arranged. If only body weight is involved with no lifting of equipment then the

Arm exercise (press-ups)

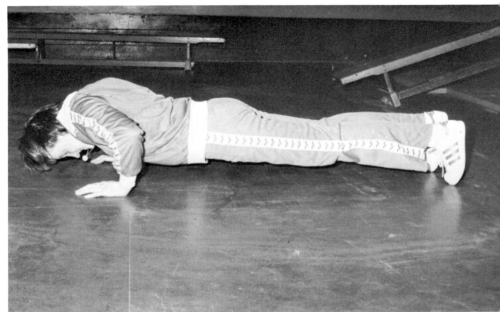

circuit will increase cardio-vascular endurance. If weights and other equipment is included then local muscular and cardio-vascular endurance can be improved. The types of activities in the cardio-vascular circuit include press-ups, squat jumps, back raising, chest raising etc., and all are done as fast as possible. In the local muscular endurance circuit similar activities are employed but with the addition of weights, for instance behind the neck in chest raises. Again these activities should be done as quickly as possible but form must be maintained in all of them. A 'good' demanding circuit will include about eight activities and each one should be worked at for about sixty seconds. When the swimmer is really fit it should be possible to go round the circuit three times with a short rest between each, giving about twenty-four minutes of all-out exercise. The exercises themselves should be placed so that an arm exercise is followed by a leg exercise then a trunk exercise and so on.

A very modern portable piece of equipment now used by many sportsmen is known as a

Leg exercise (squat jumps)

Trunk exercise (sit-ups)

  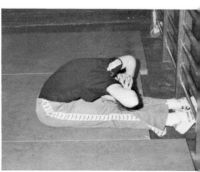

Back exercise (chest raise)

Resistance Exerciser. These small machines normally have a nylon cord running through them and usually it is possible to adjust the resistance offered by the cord as each end is held and the stroke patterns mirrored. The disadvantage of these machines is that once the resistance is set it remains constant throughout and the swimmer is unable to cope with it early and late in the pull but finds it relatively easy during the middle, stronger part of the pull. More expensive machines are available which vary the resistance throughout the stroke pattern and these are obviously more desirable. Details of all these pieces of equipment can be found in leading swimming magazines and journals.

Many sports centres, colleges, universities and schools now possess large pieces of equipment, generally known as 'Multigyms'. These exercisers can be used for both endurance and strength acquisition. They consist of a large, static, square frame to which a series of pulleys are

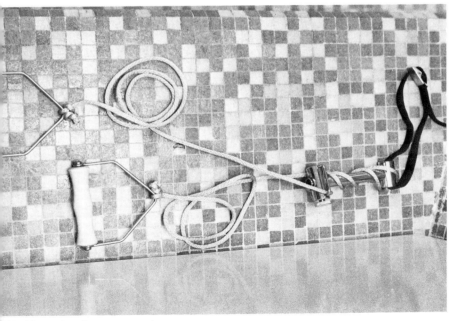

'Workhorse' resistance exerciser

Multigym

attached. Inside the frame are a large number of rectangular weights which move up and down stainless steel guides as the cords on the pulleys are moved. The pulleys are arranged so as to exercise the arms, legs, trunk and back in a number of ways. The advantage of this system is that large weights can be attempted without fear of injury from the weights toppling over or whatever. The design of the equipment allows about four or five people to work on it at the same time in a very limited space, and the weights are quickly adjusted by use of a key which saves an enormous amount of time compared with having to put weights on bars and have them lifted into place, often with the need for helpers. Strength can also be increased by weight training but the advantages of the previously mentioned methods have resulted in pure weight training for swimmers being almost completely eradicated. It is certain that swimmers need strength in very specific areas of the body. If too much bulk results in the increase of strength then the swimmer will offer more resistance to the water and could well be slower. For this reason strength

Arm station

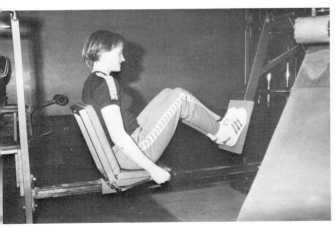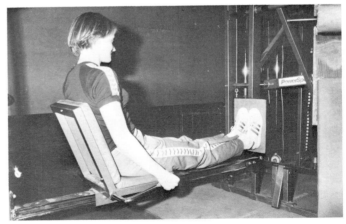

Leg station

has to be achieved very specifically and the systems which allow the exact stroke patterns to be followed should be encouraged.

In all endurance and strength training it is important that the swimmer warms up thoroughly beforehand and that the work is supervised by knowledgeable people.

Trunk and arm stations

Flexibility is an area that has been neglected by swimmers for many years. It has, however, just come back into vogue and it is quite common to see swimmers performing their mobility work before training and competition. For maximum effect, the various important joints of the body — important as far as swimming is concerned that is — must be fully extended in a gentle but firm way as often as possible. Swimmers should have a flexibility routine which extends the joints of the neck, shoulders, back, hips and ankles, all of which will play an important part in the good stroking that will be necessary for good performances. Lack of flexibility does not really become a problem until after eleven or twelve years of age; the job before that age should be aimed at increasing what flexibility is possessed because after eleven or twelve little more can be done than to maintain it. The photographs on page 95 show some of the more common exercises used for flexibility purposes.

Many swimmers will achieve great success without taking part in any land conditioning programmes. Land conditioning should not replace water conditioning but supplement it. The pressure on time for both swimmers and coach is great; consequently any land conditioning that is carefully considered to be essential should be worked at. All swimmers will need to do some flexibility work. Some will need extra strength training. If enough water time is available and the type of work already discussed used, then few swimmers will have to look for additional endurance on land.

Shoulder flexibility

 Neck and shoulder
flexibility

Trunk, side, back flexibility

Hamstring (legs) flexibility

Ankle flexibility

Tapering

Swimmers possess two aspects of water fitness — endurance and speed. One is no good without the other. The object of the whole preparation period which lasts from ten to twelve weeks is to begin by increasing the swimmer's endurance and to finish by increasing the swimmer's speed while still retaining sufficient endurance to last the distance! This final process, which involves cutting down the amount of work done and increasing the rest between the swims and the pace of them, is known as the *'tapering process'*. It is as much a psychological sharpening up as it is a physical one. As the amount of work done is reduced so the swimmer gets more rest and feels faster. This encourages the swimmer to swim faster.

Tapering a group of swimmers is a difficult task. Distance swimmers, as well as sprinters, have to be tapered. The real problem is knowing exactly when and how much to decrease the amount of work during the final few weeks before the competition. Each swimmer has to be tapered individually as some require less taper than others. If the work is cut off too soon the swimmer may show tremendous speed, but because of the fall off of endurance work may 'die' during the final stages of the race. If the swimmer's taper is too short the reverse may occur with the swimmer displaying no early speed but finishing strongly, behind the leaders! The correct taper, which can only be arrived at by experiment and experience, will allow the swimmer to show real speed early in the race and a strong finish to it also.

As a general rule the sprinters have a longer taper than the distance people because they need less endurance. Sprinters normally begin the taper from four to three weeks away from the competition. During the final week they could do as little as four or five sessions in the week which might only last for about forty-five to sixty minutes. During these sessions the sprinters might have a fairly easy warm-up followed by some legs-only work then some flat-out sprints, at race speed over 50 m and 25 m as indicated on the Chart on page 85. The session might be concluded by the sprinters spending time on starting and turning. It must be stressed that this pretty severe taper will not suit all sprinters but it is one

...d of the options available. ...ost distance swimmers work ...uite hard until about three to ...ur days before the event. It ...ould not be unusual to see ...em swimming say 15×100 m ...race pace only two weeks ...way from the competition.

...hey even swim 8×100 m or ...)×100 at race pace with only ...n to fifteen seconds rest ...during the warm-up for the ...vent. Distance swimmers ...gain will vary in their taper ...quirements and various ...pes of taper have to be ...xperimented with before the ...ne that matters is begun.

...uring the taper period the ...oach should be 'psyching' ...e swimmer up for the big ...oment. It is vital that the ...wimmer is mentally confident ...at he or she is about to ...erform better than ever before ...hen the moment arrives.

...uring these final few weeks ...e coach should aim to get ...e swimmer to perform as ...any good training swims as ...ossible. Nothing boosts ...e confidence more than ...erforming well in training. If ...e swimmer shows any real ...igns of tiredness the coach ...hould adjust the work ...ccordingly. Every good swim ...hould be highly praised by the

coach as should all the other aspects of the swim, the stroke, the starts, the turns and the pace. Swimmers will know if they are swimming well or not. The coach has to be honest with his swimmers in order to put them absolutely in the picture as to how the taper is progressing. At times extra encouragement might be necessary if a not so good swim is performed when something much better had been expected. Some swimmers will need psyching more than others. Some will be able to do the job themselves while others will require a lot of confidence-building and motivating.

Many top swimmers conclude their tapering process by 'shaving down'. This involves removing the surface hair from the arms and legs and in the case of some men the body and the head! There can be no doubt that the smoother the surfaces in contact with the water the less resistance there is. Just how much physical advantage is gained by shaving is almost impossible to measure. Its psychological benefits, however, are often enormous. It is not uncommon to hear coach and swimmer talking of reducing the best

time considerably once the swimmer has 'shaved down'. Obviously the shaving must be done under supervision and with the use of the correct cream and safety razor. It is a practice really only employed by swimmers at national and international level. What happens to the swimmer after shaving down is that on entering the water he or she will feel much 'lighter' and will experience a very pleasant tingling sensation that acts as a further stimulus to motivation, to getting the adrenalin moving around the body and to making the swimmer feel exceptionally 'different'. The shave normally takes place after the heats and before the final. During the warm-up the coach should supplement this feeling good by perhaps being a little generous with the times the swimmer records during it, although this will probably not even be necessary if the correct taper has been followed. It really is quite amazing just how much swimmers in the past have believed in the import- ance of the taper period and of shaving down, and consequently by just how much they have improved upon their best times.

Warming Up

If the 'correct' warm-up is not completed before the final of the swimmer's most important race the results could be absolutely disastrous. Defining 'correct' is the problem. As is the case throughout the sport swimmers have to be treated individually, particularly during the taper period and during the warm-up. Some swimmers, whether they are involved in a 1500 m race or a 50 m race, will need a warm-up which lasts for an hour or more and in which 3000 m or more is covered. Other swimmers in the same 1500 m or 50 m race will only need to spend fifteen or twenty minutes in the water during which time they might cover 500 or 600 m! The range really is that great.

The warm-up that is employed will depend upon what has been successful in the past.

Immediately before the most important race of a swimmer's life is not exactly the best time for experimentation. Another important factor will be how the swimmer feels during the warm-up. If the swimmer really does feel well, is in good, confident spirits and puts in some good times either on pace work or on sprints, the warm-up might well be shortened. If, on the other hand, the swimmer has not had such a good heat swim or for any other reason feels a little down, the warm-up could well be extended.

Generally speaking the warm-up should begin with a medium pace swim over 400 to 1000 m quite simply to 'wake the body up', get the circulation going a little quicker and give the swimmer a chance to settle down in what will be a very nervous period for all concerned. This swim can be done on any stroke but is normally done on freestyle with perhaps some backstroke also. Many swimmers, especially backstrokers and breaststrokers, then follow this with some legs-only work on their competition stroke. This kicking is normally begun in a gentle manner, the swimmer again trying to get the 'feel' of the water. Some sprint kicking should also take place in either some short, sharp bursts during a kick of say 200 to 400 m or more formally with say 4 or 6×50 m with about ten to fifteen seconds rest between each. The kicking work is usually followed by some medium pace full-stroke work on the competition stroke. This is to give the swimmer a chance to feel the power of the kick in he full-stroke situation. At this time the sprinters normally move on to sprint work and the distance people on to pace work. The words 'normally' and 'generally' have to be used because of what has repeatedly been said about swimmers differing in their needs so much.

The sprinters will sprint either a short series of 3 or 4×50 m or 25 m or a mixture of both. All these will be timed by the coach. Some sprinters like to try a couple of 50s first and then move on to some 25s so that the warm-up is completed at top speed. Others prefer to begin with a few 25s and end up with one or two 50s. All this work is done as near to possible at race speed although the stroke should be carefully considered with the swimmer producing excellent times with good stroke and a little in reserve. Often sprinters follow this by practising some turns in the lane in which they will appear in the final, and perhaps a few starts.

The distance swimmers should employ some pace work in their warm-up. The 1500 and 800 people usually include some pace work at 100 m

which again would be close to or exactly at race speed. The swimmer who wishes to swim the 1500 m in a time of sixteen minutes, which is an average of 1 minute 4 seconds per hundred, might do say 5 or 6×100 m with ten to fifteen seconds rest holding sixty-four seconds. The swimmer who is aiming for 9 minutes 20 seconds in the 800 m event which is an average of 1 minute 10 seconds per 100, might well do 4 or 5×100 m with ten to fifteen seconds rest and try to hold 1 minute 10 seconds. Distance swimmers do not normally work at over 100 m for pace in the warm-up but could well do say 8 or 12×50 m with five to ten seconds rest, again aiming at the average speed that is going to be necessary in order to produce the expected time. With the 1500 m swimmer looking for sixteen minutes, these 50s would have to be at around the 31–32 mark, and in the case of the 800 m swimmer hoping to do 9 minutes 20 seconds they would have to be around the 34–35 second mark. The distance swimmers often finish their warm-up with an easy swim of 200–300 m and

again might check out the turns in their final lane.

The purpose of the warm-up is to calm the swimmer down in some cases and psych the swimmer up in others. The aspects of generally getting the body warmed up and specifically getting the stroke and mind in tune, must both be stressed.

The warm-up is often followed by a light massage when the swimmer is highly susceptible to a suggestion from the coach or the masseur that this is going to be a great swim! The swimmer should keep as warm as possible after the warm-up. It helps to get some fresh air if it is not too cold and to keep fairly loose by the occasional walk. The coach will know whether a pre-race pep talk is necessary from experience. Most swimmers prefer to keep well away from their rivals immediately before the Final which will avoid any 'psyching out' that might be attempted. This is a tactic sometimes consciously, other times unconsciously, employed by swimmers of making their fellow competitors feel nervous or inferior or both! The type of talk that goes on includes the swimmer who says that he or she went really easy in the heats and was still the fastest qualifier for the final. Another favourite is the swimmer who mentions the tremendous time he or she did at some fictitious competition a few days ago. Gullible swimmers and inexperienced swimmers will allow this to affect them and will be beaten psychologically before they enter the water! The more experienced campaigners have even been known to say to their rivals that they 'look pale' or, 'what a good heat you swam but your last turn was a bit suspect'; it is amazing just how many swimmers have begun to feel a bit off colour or have made a mess of their last turn as a result of this kind of talk. This of course is not the norm but can happen—to avoid it swimmers should keep away from their rivals.

Pace Judgement

Unfortunately the shortest Olympic swimming event, the 100 m, is not a pure sprint race and does include a good deal of endurance content which calls for pace judgement. Sprinters at world-class level do not simply dive in and swim as fast as they can for as long as they can. They control the swim both in terms of stroke and pace. The 1976 Olympic Men's Freestyle Champion, Jim Montgomery of the USA, used eighteen full strokes to cover the first 50 m in 24.14 and twenty full strokes to cover the second 50 m in 25.85. The difference in number of strokes and in time between the first and second lengths is due entirely to the dive that provided the first 50 m with that advantage. The swim was, in many respects, almost an 'even pace' swim. That is to say the first half of the race is very similar to the second once the dive advantage is considered. Most world records have been established using this method of pacing which would appear to make a lot of sense both physiologically and psychologically.

The other ways of swimming the race are (i) the positive split method where the first half of the race is faster than the second, and (ii) the negative split method where the second half of the race is faster than the first.

Most young swimmers tend to swim sprint races in the positive split way. In a 100 m race held in a 50 m pool they tend to swim the first 50 m very quickly and then fade rapidly on the second 50 m. A ninety-second 100 m freestyle, backstroke or breast stroke might well be swum as forty seconds for the first 50 m and fifty seconds for the second 50 m. In a 100 m butterfly, because of its demanding nature and the extent to which the stroke breaks down under fatigue, there can be an even greater drop off. At international level the men swimming, say fifty-five seconds for the 100 m freestyle, would swim it as 26/29 seconds. The ladies swimming the same stroke and distance might swim 29/31 for sixty seconds. This then shows a difference between fifty and sixty seconds of up to three seconds. At the same level a reasonable time for men at 100 m backstroke, breast stroke and butterfly is 60 seconds, 68 seconds and 59 seconds respectively. The female equivalent times are 66, 76 and

65 seconds. In the 100 m backstroke the pace tends to be positive for both men and women. The men might swim their 60 as 29/31 and the women their 66 as 32/34. The male breaststroker swimming 68 tends to go 32/36 and the female doing 76 would do so with 36/40. It can be seen that the difference in breast stroke can be up to four seconds. The male butterflier who does 59 probably goes 28/31 compared with the girl 'flier' who might go 31/34 for her 65. Again we see a drop off of about three seconds. It is a fact, however, that the better the swimmer the less the drop off at world-class level. Indeed the current world records for men and women in all strokes at 100 m sees the smallest drop off at around the one-second mark and the greatest at around 2.5 seconds.

At 200 m the best swimmers in the world, as reflected in the world records, try to swim identical second, third and fourth 50 m. The advantage of the dive is again felt during the first 50. Again this makes the split times of the record book look like a table of positive splits. One or two examples are: men's 200 m butterfly where a good time is 2 minutes 4 seconds might be swum as 28/32/32/32 giving the first 100 m in 60 seconds and the second in 64 seconds, but the 2nd, 3rd and 4th 50 m almost identical. The women's 200 m breast stroke, where 2 minutes 40 seconds is a world-class time, might be swum as 37/41/ 41/41 giving the 100 m split at 1 minute 18 seconds and the second 100 m at 1 minute 22 seconds. Again the better the swimmer the less the drop off. The world records for the two events just mentioned have drop offs of only about one second.

At 400, 800 and 1500 m the practice of negative splitting is often employed and indeed was the way in which both the 800 m for women and the 1500 m for men were established. It would not appear to make too much sense for the second half of the swim to be faster than the first but some swimmers do prefer to swim it this way, getting into their strokes and finishing extremely strongly. It is often suggested that physiologically these swimmers could produce better overall performances by 'going out' a little faster.

However, Olympic Gold Medals and World Records do tend to speak for themselves!

Pace has to be experimented with just as work has, and so on. The necessary pace should be so ingrained in the swimmer that it really is very easy to reproduce in the race itself.

Again only by experimenting in less important races will the swimmer and coach arrive at the best way of tackling the race to be competed.

The Organisation and Running of Swimming Competitions

Reprinted by kind permission of the British Swimming Coaches Association from their annual publication 'Swim Guide'.

Planning and Preparation

Before reaching the stage of actually running a swim meet it is necessary that preliminary planning and preparation are carried out in certain areas. It is not our intention to deal with all of these aspects in detail, but we list some of them below merely as a useful check:

1. *Date*
   a. Place in Swimming Calendar
   b. Check Local and National clashes

2. *Venue*
   a. Availability
   b. Accessibility
   c. Suitability

3. *Type*
   a. Open Meet
   b. Inter-Club
   c. Championship
   d. Invitation

4. *Size of Meet*
   a. Number of competitors
   b. Number of officials
   c. Number of events and sessions
   d. Number of age groups

5. *Finance*
   a. Income
   b. Expenditure

6. *Promotion*
   Sources of income — advertising etc.

In planning any meet, careful consideration must be given to the demands to be made upon the contestants, officials, and spectators, in that order. Long, tiresome meets with too many events and/or entries, often result in poor times, poor officiating and poor public relations. Meet organising committees have an obligation to provide a setting conducive to enjoyable and stimulating competition.

Meet Sheet

This information sheet should be prepared well in advance of the actual date, and copies should be sent to all clubs and individuals who might be interested. It is a good idea for organisers to keep a mailing list which can be up-dated each year. This sheet should contain the following information.

1. *Venue*   Including main directions
2. *Date*   Number and time of sessions
3. *Length of Pool*   Number of lanes, timing system
4. *Events*

The events for both sexes and age groups (if any) should be listed on programme order. Method of determining age group, i.e. on the day of competition or by year of birth should be noted.

Where Entry Qualifying Times are required, it is usually more convenient to set these out as in the table below.

It should be indicated whether events are to be run on the 'heats and finals' or on the 'times heats, declared winner' basis. If consolation finals are to be held, this too should be indicated.

Times which will automatically gain entry should be listed and, if desired, a slightly slower time known as the Consideration Time, might also be given. This allows the organisers a degree of flexibility in ensuring both a balanced and manageable number in each event.

Any limitations on the number of events which an individual may enter, or on the number of entries permitted from one club in each event, should be clearly shown.

FRIDAY, JANUARY 6th 1978		
Women's Standard	Event	Men's Standard
4:40.85	400 m Free	4:29.54
2:59.60	200 m Breast	2:52.27
1:12.05	100 m Back	1:09.00
2:34.64	200 m I.M.	2:25.32
—	400 m Free Relay	—
SATURDAY, JANUARY 7th 1978		
2:33.82	200 m Fly	2:26.67
29.27	50 m Free	27.06
1:23.19	100 m Breast	1:18.34
2:14.88	200 m Free	2:07.05
5:27.59	400 m I.M.	5:14.52
—	800 m Free Relay	—
SUNDAY, JANUARY 8th 1978		
1:03.23	100 m Free	58.29
2:35.17	200 m Back	2:30.91
1:09.59	100 m Fly	1:04.04
9:47.00	800/1500 m Free	18:07.40
—	400 m Medley Relay	—

5. Seeding

It is strongly recommended that the proper seeding system should be used for all competitions, and this should be indicated.

6. Awards

Details of number and type of prizes for each event. Any other special awards with system of scoring, e.g. high points trophies for individuals and clubs. Again, any limitations on number of events, or number of swimmers counting for points should be shown.

7. Entry and Re-entry Procedures

The method to be used should be clearly indicated, i.e. pre-entry or poolside entry (see recommendations). Name and address of person to whom entry must be sent and closing date.

Entry fees and to whom payable. Where Consideration Times are used, notice of acceptance (with tickets) or rejection (with refunds) should be sent as soon as possible. Where Entry-Recording Cards are used all necessary information on the filling out of these should be given. Similarly, where Consolidated Entry Forms are required, these should be enclosed with full details.

8. Penalties

For failure to make entry times – the requirements and penalties associated with failure to verify entry times should be clearly outlined.

9. Recognition of Times Done

Whether the meet has been approved as a championship qualifying opportunity.

10. Warm-up Facilities

These should be shown with times. A controlled warm-up system should be used.

11. General Information

Spectators: Details of cost and availability of tickets, car parking and refreshment facilities, travel directions, availability and cost of accommodation, and useful addresses. Coaches: Special passes, and special facilities available, e.g. massage, medical, social.

Entry Standards

A. National, District and County Championship Meets

The qualifying standards for this level of competition must be progressive and challenging. In establishing entry time standards it is strongly recommended that the qualifying time be either the eighteenth or the twenty-fourth fastest time from the previous year's results or that previous year's entry standard – whichever is the faster.

B. Inter-Club Meets

It is important that when inviting clubs to participate in an Inter-Club meet, the host team should give the visiting team an indication of the level at which the meet is to be contested. This can be best done by indicating some form of time standard.

C. Open Meets

In order to limit the size of this type of meet, and shorten the length of each session, it is recommended that the organisers consider the following points in order:

1. Set entry standards (Qualifying Times)
   a. Automatic
   b. Consideration (see meet sheet details).
2. Running longer events including relays as timed finals. (Heats with declared winners.)
3. Reducing number of events. Ensure that all strokes are covered for each age group, either in one complete meet or over a series of meets.
4. Restricting individuals to a certain number of events per session.

It is important whatever the circumstances and level of competition that every effort is made to ensure that races are made competitive, i.e. swimmers of like ability participating against each other. This will guarantee that the standards improve throughout.

THE NORTHERN COUNTIES SHORT COURSE CHAMPIONSHIPS, Sharston Pool, Manchester.

MEN

NAME Please Print in Ink or Type Men	CLUB (if unattached mark unattached below)	AGE	Date of Birth	2 220 FREE	4 220 FLY	6 4 x 36 I.M.	2 110 BR/ST	4 220 BACK	6 110 FREE	2 1650 FREE	4 110 FLY	6 440 I.M.	2 440 FREE	4 110 BACK	6 220 BR/ST
			Must Complete	Saturday 12/2/77 @ 1:30 p.m. & 6:00 p.m.						Saturday 19/2/77 @ 1:30 p.m. & 6:00 p.m.					
N/Counties Time Standard				2:10	2:20	1:32	1:16.5	2:24	58.5	18:00	1:04	5:05	4:30	1:07	2:50
1															
2															
3															
4															
5															
6															
7															
8															
9															
10															
11															
12															
13															
14															
15															

THE NORTHERN COUNTIES SHORT COURSE CHAMPIONSHIPS, Sharston Pool, Manchester.

WOMEN

NAME Please Print in Ink or Type Women	CLUB (if unattached mark unattached below)	AGE	Date of Birth	1 880 FREE	3 220 FLY	5 220 BACK	1 440 FREE	3 440 I.M.	5 220 BR/ST	1 110 BACK	3 220 FREE	5 110 FLY	1 110 BR/ST	3 4 x 36 I.M.	5 110 FREE
			Must Complete	Saturday 12/2/77 @ 1:30 p.m. & 6:00 p.m.						Saturday 19/2/77 @ 1:30 p.m. & 6:00 p.m.					
N/Counties Time Standard				10:00	2:32	2:37	4:48	5:20	2:56	1:14	2:18	1:11	1:22	1:41	1:04
1															
2															
3															
4															
5															
6															
7															
8															
9															
10															
11															
12															
13															
14															
15															

ENTRY PROCEDURES

There are a number of different entry systems, and the particular one chosen will depend on the type of meet, expected numbers entering, time and facilities available etc. There are two main methods recommended: Pre-Meet or Poolside Entry.

1. Pre-Meet Entry (Large No. of Competitors)

A separate entry for each competitor in each event is completed some time in advance of the meet. The actual time allowed between the closing date of entries and the meet itself will depend on circumstances prevailing, but ideally it should be as short as possible, while allowing for administrative procedures. Although individual entry forms can be used, the 'Consolidated Entry' Form, is strongly recommended. This cuts down on paper involved, and allows easy reference. Alternatively Entry/Time Cards may be used in conjunction with Consolidated Entry forms; that is, the club or swimmer entering a competition is responsible for the pre-meet completion of the time/entry card, thus eliminating additional organisation work.

Advantages of Pre-Meet Entry Are:

- Approximate number of actual swimmers for each event is known in advance, thus allowing meet organiser to calculate length of events and session, income from entry fees etc.
- Lists of entered swimmers can be in programme.
- Provisional seeding and entry recorder cards can be prepared in advance.

Re-Entry Procedure

To facilitate smooth running of each event, as well as ensuring the most effective seeding system, competitors should be required to re-enter just prior to the start of the meet, using the already prepared entry recording cards.
A special table should be set aside in the foyer for this purpose, with labelled boxes for each event, into which the entry recording cards must be placed by a stipulated time. When it is felt necessary or desirable to have an actual programme of the heats as they will be swum, instead of merely the original entry list, then it is necessary to allow time between the re-entry process and the start of the meet for this to take place. The time required will vary with the circumstances, e.g. the previous evening.

Seeding into Heats and Lanes
can now take place.

Collection of card by swimmer. At a given time and/or by announcement swimmers must collect their individual entry recording card, which will inform them of their heat and lane number, and which they will keep with care until handed on to lane timekeeper. Where very young and inexperienced swimmers are involved, this collection may be done by the Team Manager, Coach or other accredited Official, such as Competitors' Stewards.
However, swimmers must ultimately be encouraged to take responsibility for looking after their own cards.

2. Poolside Entry

This system is best suited for local types of competition, where the entry is not likely to

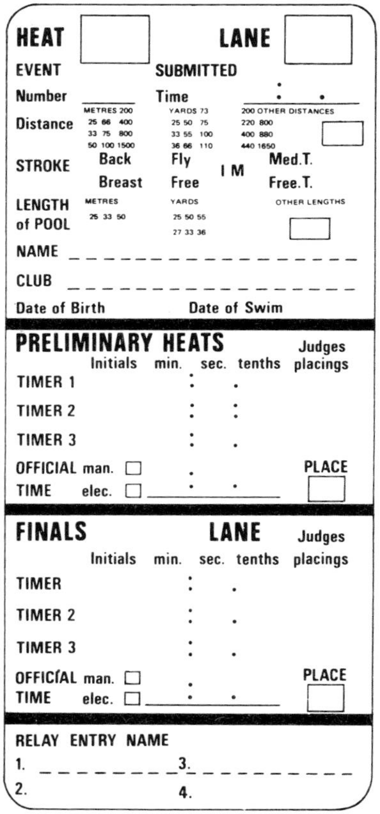

Left card (blank):

HEAT [ ]   LANE [ ]

EVENT   SUBMITTED

Number   Time   :   .

Distance   METRES 200 | YARDS 73 | 200 OTHER DISTANCES
25 66 400 | 25 50 75 | 220 800
33 75 800 | 33 55 100 | 400 880
50 100 1500 | 36 66 110 | 440 1650

STROKE   Back   Fly   Med.T.
         Breast Free   I M Free.T.

LENGTH   METRES   YARDS   OTHER LENGTHS
of POOL 25 33 50   25 50 55
                       27 33 36

NAME _ _ _ _ _ _ _ _ _ _

CLUB _ _ _ _ _ _ _ _ _ _

Date of Birth   Date of Swim

PRELIMINARY HEATS   Judges
         Initials   min.   sec. tenths placings
TIMER 1   :   .
TIMER 2   :   .
TIMER 3   :   .
OFFICIAL man. ☐   .   PLACE
TIME   elec. ☐ _____   [ ]

FINALS   LANE   Judges
         Initials   min.   sec. tenths placings
TIMER   :   .
TIMER 2   :   .
TIMER 3   :   .
OFFICIAL man. ☐   .   PLACE
TIME   elec. ☐ _____ .   [ ]

RELAY ENTRY NAME
1. _ _ _ _ _ _ _   3. _ _ _ _ _ _ _
2. _ _ _ _ _ _ _   4.

---

be large, e.g. no more than three to four heats, and where it is not felt necessary to have printed programmes.

On arrival at the pool entry-recording cards must be completed and handed in to a special entry table, in a given period of time before the start of the meet. The cards for each event are then arranged in accordance with the seeding procedure recommended, and the heats drawn up. The swimmers collect their cards, which will now show the heat and lane numbers, and report for their event, handing this card to their lane timekeepers. This system is also best used at Inter-Club and League matches where team changes often have to be made to the originally selected team.

ENTRY/TIME CARDS

These cards are available in two colours, pink for girls, blue for boys.

They can be used for all types of meets and the standard procedure for *Pre-Meet* and *Deck Entry* systems, are as follows.

Pre-Meet

The cards are filled in by the Competition organiser/Meet Manager or his Secretariat with the following information gathered from the meet information and consolidated entry sheets. Alternatively, these cards can be completed in advance by the club or swimmer concerned, and sent to the meet organiser.

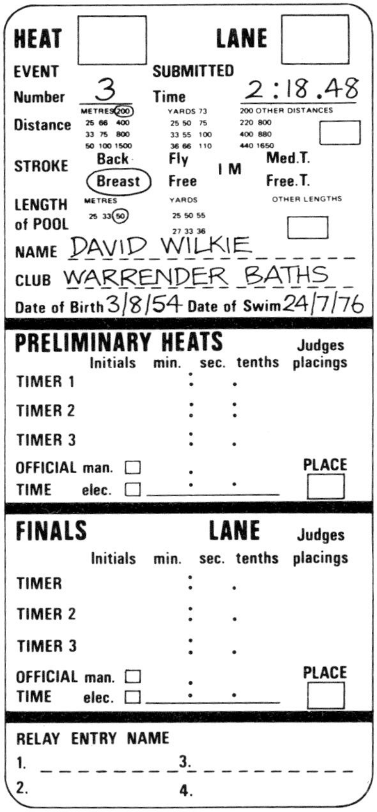

Right card (filled in):

HEAT [ ]   LANE [ ]

EVENT   SUBMITTED

Number   3   Time   2 : 18.48

Distance   METRES (200) | YARDS 73 | 200 OTHER DISTANCES
25 66 400 | 25 50 75 | 220 800
33 75 800 | 33 55 100 | 400 880
50 100 1500 | 36 66 110 | 440 1650

STROKE   Back   Fly   Med.T.
        (Breast) Free I M Free.T.

LENGTH   METRES   YARDS   OTHER LENGTHS
of POOL 25 33 (50)   25 50 55
                       27 33 36

NAME DAVID WILKIE _ _ _ _

CLUB WARRENDER BATHS _

Date of Birth 3/8/54 Date of Swim 24/7/76

PRELIMINARY HEATS   Judges
         Initials   min.   sec. tenths placings
TIMER 1   :   .
TIMER 2   :   .
TIMER 3   :   .
OFFICIAL man. ☐   .   PLACE
TIME   elec. ☐ _____   [ ]

FINALS   LANE   Judges
         Initials   min.   sec. tenths placings
TIMER   :   .
TIMER 2   :   .
TIMER 3   :   .
OFFICIAL man. ☐   .   PLACE
TIME   elec. ☐ _____ .   [ ]

RELAY ENTRY NAME
1. _ _ _ _ _ _ _   3. _ _ _ _ _ _ _
2. _ _ _ _ _ _ _   4.

This card is now ready for use

1. Event Number.
2. Submitted Time — the time submitted should be the best recorded time, or an estimated time which is slower than the best recorded time, but obviously within the entry standard for the event.
3. The Distance of the Event.

4. *The Stroke.*
5. *The Length of the Competition Pool.*
6. *The Christian and Surname of the Competitor* – in that order.
7. *The Club He or She Represents.*
8. *The Competitor's Date of Birth* – day/month/year.
9. *The Date of the Actual Swim.*

On the day of the meet the cards should be distributed to, or collected by the swimmer or team manager. The cards of those swimmers who are actually taking part, are then re-entered. This process may take place prior to the day of the meet if an actual programme of heats is required – see page 108. Consequently, the actual swimmers competing are known and, therefore, accurate seeding is much easier and empty lanes are avoided.

The seeding now takes place (see seeding procedures). Once this has been done, the *heat* and *lane* numbers can be filled in on the card.

The card is now ready to be collected by the swimmer from the recorder's table or

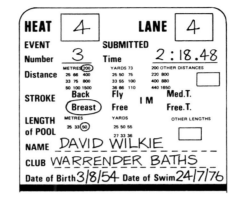

marshalling area.

N.B. In the case of very young or inexperienced swimmers, it may be advantageous to marshal them into heats and lanes before distributing the cards.

In the case of relay events, the names and order of swimmers should be listed.

It is now the swimmers' responsibility to present themselves at the start of the race with their cards and hand them to the timekeepers on the lanes indicated.

N.B. Where races are swum over an uneven number of lengths (e.g. 100 m in a $33\frac{1}{3}$ m pool) it is necessary to provide a 'runner' who will receive the cards from the swimmers and

redistribute them to the timekeepers at the opposite end of the pool.

The timekeeper will check that the competitor is in the right heat and lane and will fill in the time recorded and initial appropriately.

All relevant splits should be recorded on the reverse side. The chief timekeeper will collect the card from the lane timekeeper checking that it has been filled in correctly and initialled. He will then work out the official time.

If electronic timing is being used the chief timekeeper should take the electronic time and mark the card accordingly.

N.B. If a breakdown of the electronic timing system occurs, the official manual times can always be referred to.

The chief judge then collects all the cards and fills in the placings.

If electronic placings are being used the cards are marked accordingly.

In a case of disqualification the reason should be clearly stated on the reverse side of the form and initialled by the relevant official.

The cards are then passed to the recorder's table where the

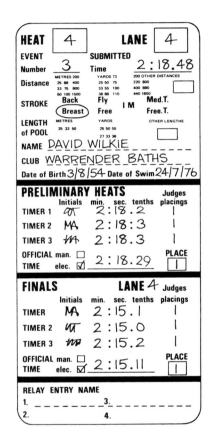

HEAT	4		LANE	4	

EVENT

Number **3** SUBMITTED Time **2 : 18.48**

Distance — METRES 200 / YARDS 73 / 200 OTHER DISTANCES:
25 66 400 | 25 50 75 | 220 800
33 75 800 | 33 55 100 | 400 880
50 100 1500 | 36 66 110 | 440 1650

STROKE — Back / Fly / Med.T. / (Breast) / Free / I M / Free.T.

LENGTH of POOL — METRES: 25 33 50 / YARDS: 25 50 55 / 27 33 36 / OTHER LENGTHS

NAME DAVID WILKIE

CLUB WARRENDER BATHS

Date of Birth 3/8/54 Date of Swim 24/7/76

PRELIMINARY HEATS

	Initials	min. sec. tenths	Judges placings
TIMER 1	GN	2 : 18.2	1
TIMER 2	MA	2 : 18 : 3	1
TIMER 3	HH	2 : 18.3	1
OFFICIAL man. ☐ TIME elec. ☑		2 : 18.29	PLACE 1

FINALS LANE 4

	Initials	min. sec. tenths	Judges placings
TIMER	MA	2 : 15.1	1
TIMER 2	GN	2 : 15.0	1
TIMER 3	HH	2 : 15.2	1
OFFICIAL man. ☐ TIME elec. ☑		2 : 15.11	PLACE 1

RELAY ENTRY NAME
1. _____ 3. _____
2. _____ 4.

results are collated. The cards of the finalists and consolation finalists are extracted and the process is then repeated for finals.

A completed Finalist's card would appear as shown. Therefore, basically the route of a time card is:

1. Competition Organiser/Meet Manager.
2. Team Manager or swimmer.
3. Competitor's Steward via entry sorting procedure.
4. Swimmer.
5. Timekeepers.
6. Chief Timekeeper.
7. Chief Judge.
8. Recorders.
9. Available to swimmers/Team Managers (for qualification purposes or TAG Ranking Lists etc.).

N.B. Time cards are available from the BSCA. Please state number and colour (blue – boys, pink – girls).

SEEDING AND PROCEDURE

Preliminary Heats

There are two different procedures – one of which should be adopted depending on the type of event.

a. Timed Heats/Declared Winner

The cards should be arranged in speed order from fastest to slowest (swimmers having the same time should be ranked by draw, not alphabetically, and swimmers without submitted times should be ranked by draw and seeded last). The cards should then be arranged into the appropriate number of heats taking into account the following:

1. The last heat must be filled before any swimmers are assigned to the second to last heat.

This principle should be followed throughout with the proviso that the first heat must contain at least *three* competitors.

2. Each heat is then arranged in the spearhead system.

b. Heats with Finals/Consolation Finals

The cards should be arranged in speed order from fastest to slowest (swimmers having the same time, or no submitted time, should be seeded as for (a)).

Swimmers should now be placed in heats in the following manner:

1. EVENTS HAVING THREE HEATS OR LESS

The fastest swimmer shall be placed in the last heat, next fastest in the second last heat, next fastest in the third last. The fourth fastest shall be placed in the last heat, fifth fastest in the second last heat, sixth fastest in the third last heat. This pattern is continued until the heats have been completed, with the proviso that no heat should contain less than three competitors, and where vacant lanes must occur, these should do so in the earlier heats.

2. EVENTS HAVING FOUR HEATS OR MORE

The last three heats (these are the fastest three heats) shall be seeded as above. The heats preceding the last three shall be seeded as for the Timed Finals (A).

A time-saving procedure when seeding heats is to lay out the time cards on a table according to the examples at the foot of this page.

FINALS/CONSOLATION FINALS

Swimmers should be assigned to lanes using the spearhead system.

N.B. A useful piece of equipment would be a previously prepared 'masterboard' to which the cards could be attached.

Duties of Officials in the Re-Entry/Time Card System

1. Competition/Meet Manager

In addition to the officials normally required by ASA Law for the running of a competition, it is recommended that there should also be a competition manager, nowadays often known as the meet manager.

His responsibilities include overall concern for the smooth and efficient running of the meet — specifically the following:

a. Sends out all information regarding the swim meet (Meet sheet), with entry forms and time cards if applicable.

b. Receives from the clubs, entry sheets and completed time cards where requested.

c. Prior to the start of the meet:

■ Produces a consolidated entry form which is filled alphabetically and kept at the scorers'/recorders' desk as a ready reference in case of an entry dispute. Where consolidated entries are required for entry, these may be used instead.

EXAMPLE: 6-LANE POOL – 32 COMPETITORS

	Lane 6	Lane 5	Lane 4	Lane 3	Lane 2	Lane 1
Heat 1				31	30	32
Heat 2		28	26	25	27	29
Heat 3	24	22	20	19	21	23
Heat 4	18	12	6	3	9	15
Heat 5	17	11	5	2	8	14
Heat 6	16	10	4	1	7	13

EXAMPLE: 8-LANE POOL – 23 COMPETITORS

	Lane 8	Lane 7	Lane 6	Lane 5	Lane 4	Lane 3	Lane 2	Lane 1
Heat 1		18	12	6	3	9	15	21
Heat 2	23	17	11	5	2	8	14	20
Heat 3	22	16	10	4	1	7	13	19

■ Ensures that the entry-
timers' cards are filled out
as follows:

First and last name of
swimmer
Full name of club
Date of birth
Date of swim
Submitted entry time
All details relating to actual
swim i.e.:
(i) events number
(ii) distance (actual
distance circled)
(iii) stroke (applicable
stroke circled)
(iv) length of pool
(applicable length
circled)
(v) passes on the time
cards to competitors'
stewards or team
managers when a re-
entry system is being
used.

N.B. For larger meets, the
manager will require a team
of helpers – secretariat.

2. Competitors' Stewards

a. Receive time card from
competition/meet manager
or team managers when a
re-entry system is being used.
b. Sort the cards into 'order of
events' (separate entry
boxes can be used for
'posting').
c. Seed using correct
procedure (and re-seed for
finals) – see recommen-
dations.
d. Ensure that time cards are
returned to the competitors
duly completed with heat
number and lane number.
■ either: (i) To individuals:
after marshalling by the
public address system one
event or more events prior
to their race. It is then the
swimmer's duty to make
sure he is at the start for
his race.
■ or (ii) To the heat as a
whole: when closer
supervision is required by
the competitors' stewards,
e.g. lower age group levels.
The system of marshalling can
be as rigid or as flexible as the
competitors' stewards allow.
e. In the case of relay events –
ensure each team member's
name is recorded prior to the
event.

3. Timekeepers

In addition to the duties
required by ASA Law:
a. Ensure swimmer is in
correct heat and lane.
b. Ensure that each timer on
the lane initials the time
card and fills in the time in
minutes, seconds, tenths.
c. Passes the time card to the
Chief Timekeeper.

4. Chief Timekeeper

In addition to the duties
required by ASA Law:
a. Collects all time cards from
each lane.
b. Completed the appropriate,
official time, as per ASA
Law.
c. Passes time cards to Chief
Judge.

5. Chief Judge

In addition to the duties
required by ASA Law:
a. Ensures that the judges'
placings are recorded on
each time card.
b. He records the competitor's
official placing.
c. Checks that the referee is in
agreement with the race
result.
d. Passes time cards to
recorders.
e. In case of disqualification
ensures that the reason for
disqualification is clearly
stated on the rear of the
time card and signed by the
relevant official.

6. *Recorder*

In addition to the duties required by ASA Law:

a. Lists the heat results in time order, fastest first, slowest last, on a result sheet, preferably typed.

b. Ensures that these results bear full name of competitors.

c. Ensures that the date of birth and age group is shown.

d. Selects appropriate numbers for finals and consolation finals, extracting appropriate cards – with alternatives (reserves) as stand by.

e. Ensures that the time cards are returned to the competitors' stewards in good time for the finals.

RECOMMENDATIONS

1. Entry Time Standards

In order to ensure equality of competition and an ever-improving standard of performance, at all levels, entry time standards should be used.

2. Failure to Achieve Required Entry Time

All swimmers who fail to achieve the required entry times must present proof within a stipulated time of having previously made that time (e.g. thirty minutes). Failure to do so should result in certain penalties being imposed. These can take various forms:

a. *Warning*

b. *Suspension* This can be more, or less, severe depending on the status of the meet, as well as the nature of the incidence of the violation, e.g. not permitted to swim in any further events in that meet, not permitted to enter the following year, not permitted to swim in any competition run by the organising body for a stated period of time.

c. *Fines* A system of fines may be levied, again on a more or less severe basis, and a sliding scale established depending on the length of the event.

N.B. In National, District and County Championships, the principles outlined under *b. Suspension* should be applied, whereas in Open Meet *c. Fines* would be more appropriate.

The Future

Swimming, above all sports, has a rapidly changing record book, even at the 100 m distances. In 1976 many world records at this distance were improved on by up to a full second. Massive amounts are knocked off world records at 1500 m and 800 m during the Major Games.

This suggests that swimming has quite a long way to go before the record books become reasonably stable. Swimmers are not necessarily spending more time training but the training is quite obviously becoming much more specific. The use of land equipment to increase strength, in previously impossible isolated areas, has been an important factor.

The medical side of the sport is being increasingly explored particularly in the areas of blood testing. Testing of this nature provides the coach with invaluable information as to how to treat the swimmer at that time. Previously this has been the area of guesswork. Psychology is also becoming vitally important and many people believe that the biggest improvement in swimming performances will come about by a better understanding of this science that will enable the coach to bring out of the swimmer the physical performance that he is capable of, but in the past has psychologically not been able to accept.

The most successful swimming nations of the world have, in some way or other, brought together the best swimmers in the country, the best coaches in the country and placed them in the best facilities available.

This grouping of real excellence has brought tremendous results to those countries that have really done the job well. It is quite clear that if any other nations are to appear on the world scene that they in some way or other will have to organise themselves along these lines. In all cases the education of the people concerned will have to be carefully planned to prevent swimmers and coaches from beginning their day at 5 a.m. and finishing at 8 p.m. because swimming training can only take place before work or school, and after it, which tend to be inflexible times. Professional coaches are now the norm and not the exception, and good coaches will attract swimmers from a very wide area and will also result in some families actually moving house to be near to a good club and coach.

The rewards of this well-structured sport have been discussed. The advantages to be gained by young people participating in the sport are obvious.

When the swimmer's competitive days are over there is an enormously varied and interesting field that can be followed in the teaching, coaching, administrative and officiating sides of the sport. It is hoped that every swimmer will consider in what way he or she can put something back into this sport of swimming from which they have gained so much.